THE PRACTITIONER INQUIRY SERIES

Marilyn Cochran-Smith and Susan L. Lytle, Series Editors

(continued)

D0840010

Family Dialogue Journals

School–Home Partnerships That Support Student Learning

JoBeth Allen, Jennifer Beaty, Angela Dean,
Joseph Jones, Stephanie Smith Mathews,
Jen McCreight, Elyse Schwedler, & Amber M. Simmons

From the Red Clay Writing Project

Foreword by Luis C. Moll

TEACHERS COLLEGE PRESS
TEACHERS COLLEGE | COLUMBIA UNIVERSITY
NEW YORK AND LONDON

NATIONAL WRITING PROJECT
BERKELEY, CA

Published simultaneously by Teachers College Press, 1234 Amsterdam Avenue, New York, NY 10027 and the National Writing Project, 2105 Bancroft Way, Berkeley, CA 94720-1042

The National Writing Project (NWP) is a nationwide network of educators working together to improve the teaching of writing in the nation's schools and in other settings. NWP provides high-quality professional development programs to teachers in a variety of disciplines and at all levels, from early childhood through university. Through its network of nearly 200 university-based sites, NWP develops the leadership, programs and research needed for teachers to help students become successful writers and learners.

Library of Congress Cataloging-in-Publication Data is available at loc.gov

ISBN 978-0-8077-5628-7 (paper)
ISBN 978-0-8077-5629-4 (hardcover)
ISBN 978-0-8077-7364-2 (ebook)

Printed on acid-free paper
Manufactured in the United States of America

22   21   20   19   18   17   16   15   8   7   6   5   4   3   2   1

Contents

Foreword

It was with great interest that I read *Family Dialogue Journals*, which describes a novel way of establishing communications and fruitful social relations among teachers, students, and parents for pedagogical purposes. And it is a pleasure to write this foreword for a book that spotlights teachers' transformative practices. That the work was inspired, at least in part, by our research on funds of knowledge is most satisfying. And indeed, the Family Dialogue Journals (FDJs) work shares several principles with the funds of knowledge approach—namely, establishing social relations with families that come to serve as assets for instruction, thus creating favorable and useful representations of families and students. But as in other such projects, there are changes in methods and practices as ideas are adapted, as well they should be, to various local circumstances that include different situations, constraints, and affordances.

When my colleagues and I initiated the studies based on the idea of funds of knowledge, conducted in Tucson, Arizona, we designed the project as a collaborative venture with teachers (González, Moll, & Amanti, 2005). We modeled the design on a study with a similar ethnographic intent of learning from the families, but with a focus on home literacy practices that Stephen Díaz, Henry Trueba, and I had conducted previously with a dozen or so teachers in San Diego, California (e.g., Moll & Diaz, 1987). However, we had to make strategic adjustments for the work in Tucson. At first, and as in San Diego, the university-based researchers conducted the household visits and shared the findings with the teachers in a biweekly study group at which we would discuss pedagogical innovations based on what we were learning collectively. In Tucson, the teachers did accompany us during our first household visit to the homes of their students, and we were impressed by how well and willingly the families received us. These were obviously special visits, and the teachers were honored guests. We benefited greatly from the mutual respect displayed during those visits, which made it much easier to earn the families' trust and facilitated greatly our subsequent research visits to their households.

It took us only a few visits to realize that the teachers would make insightful household researchers. We modified our design in subsequent studies so that teachers could participate as co-researchers, collecting their own firsthand data for analysis and interpretation, in case-study fashion, rather than relying on any secondhand information we could provide. It also made the relation between teachers and researchers much more symmetrical; the teachers could now reason and argue based on their own data. The study groups with teachers, which is also an important feature of FDJs, became a special setting, a "mediating structure," as I have called it—a space for presenting and reflecting on findings, developing a common theoretical vocabulary, solving logistical problems, and conceptualizing and scrutinizing any instructional innovations that resulted from our joint documentation of funds of knowledge (Moll, 2014). These study-group settings also became a place to address ethical issues and watch out for damaging stereotypes, which are abundant, especially regarding low-income families and children. No one is immune to these stereotypes and to related social and language ideologies; they are always in the air. As JoBeth Allen and colleagues write, their best advice is "to reflect constantly, seeking to recognize the inherent power differentials in the ways that society and institutions and we as teachers position families, teachers, and students" (p. 4). This point is indeed well taken.

Rather than conducting household visits, the FDJ participants, in varied ways depending on the teacher, used the frequency and openness of written exchanges to establish the relationships that led to integrating parental and student interests, experiences, and opinions into each classroom's academic agenda. A key to the work was the openness of the communications, as they write: "We asked students and families to share personal details about their lives, experiences, and opinions. It would not be a true dialogue if we were not willing to do the same, and therefore, the openness of the teacher in her responses was integral to the implementation of FDJs" (p. 27). This form of communication is difficult, as they acknowledge, and it requires tact and authenticity but also candor—not an easy combination. It also has its risks and, as such, must be monitored carefully. It is easy to misunderstand intent in written communications, as users of email can readily attest, and this is a problem. Therefore, the development of *confianza*, as we call it in Spanish— the sort of mutual trust central to conducting household visits—also became important in exchanging written messages and in creating frank and useful communications. But what is most powerful is that one can come to think of FDJs not only as tools for facilitating communications and enhancing trust but also as tools for generating new funds of knowledge for all participants about family life, cultural practices, student interests, and academic routines and activities. This is quite an achievement.

The diversity of teacher experiences in using FDJs but also their resounding success in creating a social matrix for learning and advancement in school are also impressive achievements. The use of FDJs created a dynamic model system that supported the students academically, while personalizing the relationships among participants. Family members who did not write in English were encouraged to correspond in their home language and, whenever necessary, students or other teachers and community members helped with translations. The students and parents became, we could say, *subjects* instead of simply *objects* of learning; in many ways the FDJs helped the participants cocreate the teaching and learning activities in each classroom setting. The collective work of these educators, rather than simply seeking to accommodate the students to existing didactic practices, came to challenge the status quo in these different classroom settings by offering alternatives that were both meaningful and rigorous for all participants.

There is definitely much to learn in the pages that follow.

—Luis C. Moll

REFERENCES

González, N., & Moll, L. C., & Amanti, C. (Eds.). (2005). *Funds of knowledge: Theorizing practices in households, communities, and classrooms*. Mahwah, NJ: Erlbaum.

Moll, L. C. (2014). *L. S. Vygotsky and education*. London, England: Routledge.

Moll, L. C., & Diaz, S. (1987). Change as the goal of educational research. *Anthropology & Education Quarterly, 18*(4), 300–311.

CHAPTER 1

Why Use Family Dialogue Journals?

> Now is the time to transform family engagement strategies so that they are intentionally aligned with student learning and achievement.
>
> —Heather Weiss, M. Elena Lopez, and Heidi Rosenberg, *Beyond Random Acts: Family, School, and Community Engagement as an Integral Part of Education Reform*

Jen McCreight's 1st-grade students spread out across the room, some at desks, some on their bellies on the rug, all writing in new black-and-white composition books. Jen rotated around the room, conferencing with students on the question they had constructed together to ask the children's families, "What are your hopes and dreams for me this year?" She stopped to write "*¿Cuales son sus sueños y esperanzas para mí?*" in Naldo's journal, as his family primarily spoke Spanish. Naldo's writing already consisted of multiple sentences about his dream of learning to drive a car. Her eyes widened when she realized he was writing entirely in Spanish. He was a fearless speller, stretching out the sounds he heard, e.g., "keyro" for "*quiero.*"

"My mom wants me to learn Spanish and English this year," Naldo explained. She will teach me to read in Spanish and I will teach her English, because she doesn't know much English yet and she wants me to help her learn."

The following Monday during Morning Meeting, as students shared what they and their family members had written about 1st-grade hopes and dreams, Jen highlighted Naldo's entry and encouraged other students to write to their families in *their* home language. Several did. In a school with 69% Spanish-speaking families and no biliteracy instruction, the students created their own curriculum, learning from their families through Family Dialogue Journals (FDJs).

Ninety miles away in a large urban school district, Angela Dean's 9th-grade students and their families wrote about the masks people sometimes wear. They were studying issues the characters faced in the novel *Bronx Masquerade* by Nikki Grimes. Julian considered in what ways he wore masks like the characters of the book.

Julian: Dear Mother, In literature we've been reading a book called Bronx Masquerade. It's about high school students and each chapter is a different student. The students talk about their life, discuss problems, and then write a poem that reflects on them or somebody they know. Most students in this society wear masks. Metaphorically speaking. Meaning they act one way around others and feel another way inside. But most students act like this because they are different and feel like they don't fit in their surroundings. I feel like this sometimes when there are a lot of tall people around me and other times when I'm the only black person around. Have you ever felt different in a way or not accepted by others?

Julian's mother: Being the only girl growing up in a house full of boys and the youngest of four, I always felt different because I was a girl and was told I would not play football or box. They always told me that I was too young to play or do certain things so I never felt like I belonged until I found my own friends.

Angela: I can relate. When I was young, a boy told me I couldn't be a football player. I argued, but he was adamant—no girls could play football. I went home and told my mom. She told me that I needed to go back and tell him I could be anything I wanted. I did. He still didn't agree. I've often felt that I had more to prove with my guy friends—I competed against them in classes when it came to grades. I didn't want to seem dumb. A lot of girls tended to play the whole airhead routine, but I wanted to be seen as smart and equal.

This Family Dialogue Journal sequence allowed Julian to critically examine how he saw himself in society. In response, his mother and Angela, as women, were able to validate his sense of inadequacy when around those different from himself. Angela saw entries such as this as promoting her goals (and those of the Common Core State Standards) for developing argument writing, considering multiple perspectives, and expanding critical thinking.

THE RATIONALE FOR FAMILY DIALOGUE JOURNALS

We teach in a time when standards dictate most school decisions. Teachers spend a significant part of their day teaching students what they are going to learn, why they are learning it, and how they will know when they have "mastered" the learning. Parents are increasingly bewildered, marginalized, and sometimes even angry—witness the reaction in the blogosphere from parents to the Common Core standards (National Governors

Association Center for Best Practices & Council of Chief State School Officers, 2010). With more and different skills required of students and teachers, parents need to know what their children are learning, and this does not mean being referred to the Common Core website or given a handout at the beginning of the year with a list of the standards covered in that grade. Instead, what if parents *really* knew what was going on and what if there were an ongoing dialogue among themselves, their child, and the teacher?

In "Rethinking Title 1 Parental Involvement: Moving Beyond a Checklist of Activities to a Systemic Plan for Sustained Family and Community Engagement," U.S. Department of Education officials Bega, Johnson, and Jasper (2012, n.p.) emphasized reenvisioning parent and community involvement. That vision for sustained family and community engagement calls for "the systemic inclusion of parents and families as partners with local educational agencies and school staff in their child's education in a manner that promotes shared responsibility for student learning"; involvement opportunities that are "responsive to student, parent, and family needs"; and building of a relationship that "reinforces that learning begins at birth and takes place in the home, school, and community." From analyzing parental involvement research Bega and colleagues concluded that effective involvement "means the participation of parents in regular, two-way, and meaningful communication involving student academic learning and other school activities," including ensuring that "parents play an integral role in assisting their child's learning [and] are encouraged to be actively involved in their child's education at school."

MEANINGFUL CONNECTIONS WITH COMMON CORE STANDARDS

- Students can teach a family member a new math strategy such as expanded form for multiplying or partial quotients when dividing.
- Encourage a family debate using argumentative writing skills about a science or social studies topic.
- Students and family member(s) engage in "close reading" of an article or excerpt from a novel together and make annotations in the journal about their reading experience. They can include insights, connections, and further wonderings.
- Using the scientific method, student and family member(s) respond to a science experiment conducted at home or in school. This could be in relation to the student's science fair project.
- Bring history to life by interviewing a member of the family or community about his or her experience during Japanese internment, September 11, or any other social studies topic or current event.

This conclusion is borne out by rigorous analysis of 80 studies on parental involvement programs and practices, prekindergarten through high school throughout the United States, conducted by Anne Henderson and Karen Mapp (2002). Overall, they found, "The evidence is consistent, positive, and convincing: many forms of family and community involvement influence student achievement at all ages" (p. 7) *and across economic and cultural groups*. Three of their major research findings guided our work. Across studies, family engagement that led to increased student learning had the following characteristics:

- Family involvement invitations were *linked to student learning*.
- Family involvement invitations *supported student learning at home*.
- Educators built *respectful relationships* with all families.

As we designed, discussed, and analyzed what happened in our implementation of FDJs, we used these tenets as a touchstone. First, did student–family–teacher interactions in the journals connect learning at school with learning at home? We tried to make this a two-way bridge, not only sharing classroom learning at home, but soliciting and incorporating family knowledge into the curriculum. Second, did we provide ways for families to support their children at home without imposing school norms on family life? Frankly, we struggled with this one. There were times when we read our own words and cringed a little bit—had we inappropriately exerted power over children? Over families? Probably. Our best advice, to ourselves and to our readers, is to reflect constantly, seeking to recognize the inherent power differentials in the ways that society and institutions and we as teachers position families, teachers, and students.

And finally, were the relationships we built with families respectful and reciprocal? We asked ourselves this third question with a deep commitment to learning and incorporating family funds of knowledge (Gonzáles, Moll, & Amanti, 2005). Adopting a funds-of-knowledge stance involves a shift from thinking about what families "don't/can't/won't do" to what families do, how they do it, and how children learn with and from their families. Family funds of knowledge may include work in and out of the home, religious and cultural traditions, home and vehicle repair, child care, medicine, language and knowledge of home country, musical ability, entrepreneurial ventures, and more than we could have imagined before we began the FDJs. Gonzáles and colleagues learned family funds of knowledge through developing out-of-school relationships at ball games and religious and family events, and, primarily, through family (home) visits. Many of us participated in such face-to-face interactions regularly. But we wanted a more consistent avenue for dialogue with families—dialogue that focused on student learning.

BENEFITS OF FAMILY DIALOGUE JOURNALS

- Families connect to life in the classroom.
- Family voices contribute to curriculum.
- Teachers extend curriculum through authentic sources of cultural and linguistic diversity.
- Students learn about their families' experiences and opinions.
- Students develop multiple perspectives and broaden their learning.
- Students who speak more than one language develop biliteracy.
- Students, families, and teachers deepen relationships.
- Students apply content and process knowledge outside of school.
- Classroom community strengthens with and beyond school walls.
- Students build confidence in speaking and listening through sharing.
- Students develop narrative, informative, and persuasive writing abilities.
- Teachers provide writing craft lessons for authentic communication.
- Students refine questioning skills, develop critical literacy, and engage in social-justice issues in their lives and in their community.

This book is about our development, implementation, and inquiry into Family Dialogue Journals, a "regular, two-way, and meaningful communication involving student academic learning" that seeks to be "responsive to student, parent, and family needs" (Bega et al., 2012). The project grew out of our own needs, previous experiences, and dissatisfaction with what often "counts" as "parental involvement" (showing up at the school). It also grew out of what we learned from other teachers and families.

WHAT HAVE OTHER TEACHERS DONE?

We learned about the power of parent–teacher–student dialogue from Betty Shockley (now Bisplinghoff) and Barbara Michalove, who had years earlier invited JoBeth into their 1st and 2nd grades at the time (Shockley, Michalove, & Allen, 1995). Parents and others in their African American and European American working-class community sustained a remarkable commitment to read with their children, talk about the books, and write together in "reading journals" two to three times a week all year long. Betty and Barbara responded to every entry during their planning periods.

Families established their own styles and uses of the journal. They talked about stories, illustrations, family values, what they learned, their children's literacy development, and the concerns that fill every family's life. This extended written dialogue, not about discipline problems or signing agendas, established deep relationships. It also supported emerging readers and writers in ways neither teacher nor parent could have alone. For example, LaToya's mom appreciated sharing books that gave them the opportunity to talk about their African American heritage:

> LaToya read, "Follow the Drinking Gourd." I enjoyed this book with LaToya. I am glad she is finding books to read about her own people. She asked me a lot of questions about slaves and white people and why they hate each other, and why she should be proud to be black. She had so many questions it took us 1 ½ hours to read this book and for me to explain things to her. Mary (quoted in Shockley et al., 1995, p. 72)

Journals often became a site of collaborative literacy support. Parents suggested that teachers send home books that were harder, or easier, or had more words. Teachers suggested that parents try reading a difficult book to the child first, then listening to the child read. They discussed complexities such as the difficulty of comprehending when the child was spending so much energy on decoding. Parents who had not completed high school regularly shared thoughtful insights because they were invited into a genuine dialogue in which teachers respected their opinions and suggestions.

Our thinking also benefitted from our colleagues Amy Kay (pre-K and kindergarten), Andrea Neher (1st), and Lindsey Lush (3rd and 5th), who implemented "home–school journals" (Kay, Neher, & Lush, 2010). Through weekly journal exchanges, these teachers gained insights about student learning at home, family support, and listening to families. For example:

- Amy learned from one child's mother, "Our favorite hobby is collecting movies. So whatever family title she can read, sometimes with some help, she can watch before bedtime. Now we rent more subtitle movies, and she tries to keep up with each dialogue. I also ask her about hair products. Reading the labels are becoming more common now than just grabbing a familiar bottle" (p. 419).
- One of Andrea's students was worried about the upcoming state test. His mother wrote, "Anywho fella, no matter how you feel about the CRCT [Georgia's standardized test], I want you to do your absolute best. If you plan on becoming the President of The United States of America, doing great on this test is the best start for reaching your dreams" (pp. 420–421).
- Lindsey initially had a different vision for the journals than parents did. She intended to focus on building relationships and on academic content. Parents, however, wrote with obvious concern about academic struggles, school attendance, homework and classwork. Lindsey realized, "This could be the first time

these families were feeling like participants in the child's school experience, rather than just receivers of information" (p. 423).

One of us, Stephanie, worked closely with school colleague Andrea Neher, whose whole grade level used home-school journals (Kay, Neher, & Lush, 2010). Stephanie mused,

> Because she was at my same school, I couldn't use the excuses, "Not everyone speaks English and I *only* speak English, parents will be too busy with jobs and kids and life to participate, I'm too busy with other requirements and mandates." However, I still wondered, "Well, what about students who speak another language? Will parents have the time and/or interest in these journals? How can these journals help me teach the curriculum I am required to teach?" The benefits I saw in Andrea's class seemed to outweigh potential barriers. I decided to give it a try. I thought that these journals had the potential to help my students form deeper connections with their families, classmates, and the curriculum. I also thought that these journals would help me form deeper relationships with my students and their families. I was right.

Our secondary teachers Joseph, Angela, and Amber were especially impressed by Damion Frye (2009), a 9th-grade teacher in New York City. He taught a required World Literature course in a culturally diverse school and was disturbed that most of his students were failing. He decided to enlist the support of parents by implementing "Parent Journals" ten times a semester. On those Fridays, students wrote in their journals for 10 minutes on a prompt from Damion, e.g., "define tragedy," "respond to the poem," or "extend a storyline." Students took the journals home, and it was their responsibility (and part of their grade) to discuss the assignment with a parent or another adult. The adult either responded to the same topic or responded to their child's writing. Damion responded by writing in each by the following Friday—100 students!

He reported that 85% of his students responded almost every week, and 13% responded at least once. Damion wrote, "This was an arduous task, but certainly one of the most fruitful and rewarding of my career." Most students, initially "aghast that their parents would now be required to read and respond to their journals," eventually saw the benefits; every one passed the course. One student commented, "I like the parent journal because it is the only time my father and I talk." Damion concluded, "Parents have been much more involved with their child's education and subsequently *almost all of the students' academic performances dramatically increased.*" It was especially gratifying that parents who spoke English as a second language and parents of "underskilled" students expressed how valuable the home journals were. After analyzing 3 years' worth of data, Frye concluded:

First, the more often a parent reads and responds to her child's thinking and writing, the more quickly the child improves in thinking and writing about texts. Second, by including parents even in the most simplistic manner, I was able to create allies within the larger parent community; this helped me achieve my goal of having each of my students earn a 70% or above. Last, the journal created an academic environment in the children's homes; they could no longer hide their work in their backpacks or refuse to show their writing to their parents.

Angela saw many connections between Frye's students and her college preparatory classes. "I felt an urgency to use the journals in my 10th-grade classroom because parental involvement was lower and the failure rate higher than in Honors or AP classes," she explained. "I wanted to bridge home and school in my CP World Literature course. Studying various cultures of the world and ignoring the rich cultures of students seemed like teaching blindfolded." Students were often just expected to see connections between the literature and their lives; Angela wanted to make the connection explicit by bringing in the experiences and opinions of families. She wanted parents and students to enter a dialogue with one another and with her surrounding the issues raised in the texts the class explored.

Angela hoped that valuing parent involvement in this way and tapping into family funds of knowledge would shift the interactions she had with parents and students toward meaningful learning and away from what many parents had come to expect: meetings in which teachers aired the long list of failures on the part of the child while the parent listened patiently, nodding and saying that it wasn't the first time they've heard these concerns. Many talked of feeling at a loss as to what to do with their child and how to motivate them to meet the demands of school. Family Dialogue Journals offered a radical shift in that negative dynamic.

Collectively and individually, we read practical summaries (e.g., Allen, 2007, 2010) and action research on dialogue journals (e.g., Wollman-Bonilla, 2000). Amber (Simmons, 2013) learned from her review of the literature that while little has been written about three-way journals in high school, secondary educators have for decades recommended teacher–student dialogue journals to (1) provide authentic audiences for writers, (2) engage more deeply in literature discussions, (3) help scaffold student understanding, and (4) support English learners' fluency and knowledge of language structures. We continue to find pertinent scholarship (e.g., Rowe & Fain, 2013) and to learn both the possibilities and the limitations from other teachers and researchers.

And finally, we found that the instruction before FDJ entries, thought processes during their creation, learning from families as they respond, and sharing of multiple perspectives from the journals address an impressive number of local, state, and national standards, including Advanced Placement and Common Core standards (see sidebars for elementary and secondary examples). Some of us addressed specific standards in mini-lessons. For example, we taught writing standards related to conventions and organization in order for our families to understand our writing; Social Studies standards related to geography, maps, and culture; and English Language Arts standards comparing texts to other texts or world events. Students learned to listen and speak with one another and teachers in a collaborative and respectful manner throughout the process of generating writing ideas at the beginning of each cycle and sharing their families' responses at the end of a cycle. Students contributed ideas from their learning, presented information from their families, and asked and answered questions orally to better understand family responses. We addressed standards across the curriculum as students applied reading, researching, writing, listening, and speaking skills to discuss their learning in multiple content areas.

ELEMENTARY ENGLISH LANGUAGE ARTS LITERACY STANDARDS

CCSS.ELA-Literacy.SL.1.1 & 2.1. Participate in collaborative conversations with diverse partners about grade 1/grade 2 topics and texts with peers and adults in small and larger groups.

CCSS.ELA-Literacy.SL.3.1 & 4.1 & 5.1. Engage effectively in a range of collaborative discussions with diverse partners on grade 3 topics/grade 4 topics/grade 5 topics and texts, building on others' ideas and expressing their own clearly.

CCSS.ELA-Literacy.SL.1.3. Ask and answer questions about what a speaker says in order to clarify comprehension, gather additional information, or clarify something that is not understood. (Plus at subsequent grade levels: deepen understanding of a topic or issue [2.3]; offering appropriate elaboration and detail [3.3])

CCSS.ELA-Literacy.W4.4 & 5.4. Produce clear and coherent writing in which the development and organization are appropriate to task, purpose, and audience.

CCSS.ELA-Literacy.W.3.10 & 4.10. Write routinely over extended time frames (time for research, reflection, and revision) and shorter time frames (a single sitting or a day or two) for a range of discipline-specific tasks, purposes, and audiences.

CCSS.ELA-Literacy.W.1.1. Write opinion pieces in which they introduce the topic or name the book they are writing about, state an opinion, supply a reason for the opinion, and provide some sense of closure.

CCSS.ELA-Literacy.W.1.2. Write informative/explanatory texts in which they name a topic, supply some facts about the topic, and provide some sense of closure.

HIGH SCHOOL LANGUAGE ARTS STANDARDS (BASED ON COMMON CORE)

- Use textual evidence; summarize; determine themes; analyze character development; question stylistic choices; use context clues; recognize how language adds to meaning; understand elements of structure; understand irony, satire, and understatement; understand that texts have multiple interpretations.
- Write arguments to support claims in an analysis of substantive topics using valid reasoning, effective organization, relevant and sufficient evidence, sophisticated vocabulary, and varied sentence structure.
- Demonstrate command of Standard English, including spelling, punctuation, and capitalization; understand the functionality of language; pay special attention to vocabulary.
- Draw evidence from literary and informational texts to support analysis; evaluate reasoning of texts; incorporate information while maintaining fluidity in writing; evaluate reasoning of texts; gather information from multiple authorities.
- Engage in discussions with peers and teacher; use text as evidence when questioning, providing opinion, or defending point of view; respect others' point of view; recognize fallacies, faulty logic, and distorted evidence.

ETHICAL AND LOGISTICAL CONCERNS

There is no ideal school or class or teacher for which Family Dialogue Journals work perfectly all the time—including ours. A student will inevitably forget to bring the journal back, or a parent will be too busy to respond, or a teacher will leave a journal at home or "lose" it under the seat of the car, or if you're like us, all of the above. Multiple times. Each year. When we heard from families or observed in the classroom that something wasn't working, we talked with students and made changes, as you will read about throughout the book. The process doesn't have to be perfect for the journals to have an impact in the classroom.

Sometimes students didn't write, or didn't take their journals home, or didn't share with their parents, or didn't bring them back. Sometimes we weren't able to find out why. School pressures can overwhelm teachers, and family emergencies can make responding in the journal a low priority. In one classroom, 11 out of 16 children returned from the winter holiday dealing with deportation, divorce, abuse, and other serious issues. Some students didn't share their journals with parents because they felt they needed to protect their parents; others just didn't relate to their parents this way and didn't want to talk with them about school. In some classrooms students are pulled out for so many services that they were only able to write occasionally.

As teachers, we recognize that each student's situation is unique. We often talked with children and family members to figure out what was hindering the journal-writing process and what could be done. For instance, a student of Stephanie's was in foster care and didn't feel comfortable sharing his journal with his foster family at first. He was, however, very fond of the school counselor, so Stephanie helped him work out a schedule for sharing the journal with the counselor. It proved to be a beneficial experience for the student to build trust with an adult whom he respected. He was then able to feel included in the class process and he eventually began sharing his journal with his foster parents. In Amber's classroom, one student did not turn in his FDJ. When Amber inquired, he said that he did not want her to read his mother's response. Because he trusted Amber, he informed her that his mother had a mental illness and that her response was incoherent and did not address the FDJ question/prompt. Amber told the student to remove his mother's response from the journal if he was uncomfortable with her reading it and the two discussed the possibility of sharing the journal with other family members or close friends. Amber and the student agreed that his grandmother would be a good choice. Another of Amber's students had his best friend occasionally contribute to his FDJ because his mother, a single parent, traveled for work and was sometimes unavailable to write in the journal. Encouraging students to articulate and solve problems shows the student that you respect the situation, care about the journal process, and want to help find a solution that will work best for all involved. Extending the pool of individuals who can contribute to the FDJs helped make the process more accessible to more students. Even when some of our students and/or parents didn't write consistently, the dialogue between student and teacher was often meaningful and the insights that other students shared encouraged those who were reluctant to engage.

As these examples show, logistical and ethical issues overlap. We are acutely aware that asking parents to participate in the FDJ process entails multiple ethical considerations, and we discussed these issues at our monthly meetings. We discussed research by Curt Dudley-Marling (2009) and colleagues, who interviewed 18 African American and 14 immigrant parents of English learners in two urban communities to learn their perceptions of home–school reading practices. Parents identified many efforts the schools made to get their children to read at home and various forms of documentation the school requested, such as signing reading logs. Parents revealed insightful critiques of the most common request: "just read." Some parents were concerned that (a) their children did not enjoy forced reading time, (b) they didn't see a role for themselves beyond surveillance, and (c) when they asked how they could help their children, they were told to just have them read more. Interestingly, some viewed "just reading" as additional work that actually interfered with required homework that they viewed as more important because teachers graded it. Dudley-Marling identified a cultural gap between the family values and expectations and those of the schools. He concluded that "a family literacy considerate of the cultural and material lives of families and committed to the academic achievement of all students must seek better understanding of home literacy practices and how to build on those practices in support of school learning" (Dudley-Marling, 2009, n.p.).

We realize that we, too, imposed a school practice on families by asking them to write in the FDJs. However, we did seek and respond to family input in a variety of ways: by framing the journals as an invitation to be actively involved in their child's learning; by asking families how the process was working for them, talking with families in person and by phone initially and when we were concerned; and by opening the door to dialogue weekly through the journals themselves.

Amber identified another ethical issue. She noted that the journals amplified her emotional response, because she was so much closer to the families. She also worried about betraying the students' trust. What do you do when the journals reveal that kids are hurting because of something happening at home? One student told her that the journal was revealing that his mother might be having a relapse of her paranoia; the writing had become rambling and disjointed. They agreed to rip his mother's pages out at the end, and he could use those to document the help that she might need. He raised serious questions, and Amber wasn't sure how to respond. Does he need to stay home with his mother instead of going to college, is it hereditary, will his children have a relationship with their grandmother?

We address concerns such as these throughout this book. Our point here is that we know we are not suggesting a simple, value-free technique to help students learn. FDJs are a radically different way of forming partnerships with families, radical in the sense that this kind of communication gets "at the root" of relationships based on reciprocity and *confianza*—mutual trust (Gonzáles et al., 2005). So who are we, and how did we come to this radical practice?

FDJ STUDY GROUP PROCESS

All of us are Red Clay Writing Project Teacher Consultants. We formed a study group to share our FDJ experiences and learn from one another. During the first year of the FDJ Study Group we posted our experiences, challenges, family responses, and frustration on a wiki and responded to one another with suggestions, encouragement, and empathy. We met each month face to face to read from the journals, brainstorm curricular connections, and support one another in problem solving. The second year, we began analysis and continued implementation for those continuing in the classroom (we had several life and career changes). By the third year, we were ready to write.

For Jen, the group was a sounding board, patiently allowing her the space to work through hiccups in her own implementation of the journals and providing her with suggestions when she was stuck. Additionally, when her FDJ colleagues discussed their successes and difficulties, Jen incorporated the threads of their experiences into her own classroom, enhancing and strengthening her students' experience as she learned from and with her peers. Amber described the FDJ support/study group as a resource through which she could share her successes and challenges and receive feedback from colleagues who were also implementing family dialogue journals. In this way, she was able to compare her struggles and triumphs to what others were facing and employ techniques that were working in their classrooms. Amber found that the support of a professional community was essential to her self-reflection and that members of the group encouraged her when she was frustrated and celebrated when she thrived.

INTRODUCING OURSELVES AND OUR CLASSROOMS

At the time of this writing, we had variously implemented Family Dialogue Journals from 1 to 3 years in our Title 1 classrooms, with some of us changing grade levels during the study. We were currently or had previously been in graduate programs in Language and Literacy Education at the University of Georgia, where JoBeth teaches. We introduce ourselves here, concluding with a demographics chart (Table 1.1) to help you keep us straight.

Jen McCreight, Kindergarten Class That Looped to 1st Grade

As a kindergarten and 1st-grade teacher for 8 years, Jen worked with children from diverse socioeconomic, linguistic, racial, ethnic, and familial backgrounds. A European American, middle-class educator who primarily taught Latin@ and African American students, Jen knew she needed to learn more about her students and their families in order to create a community of learners who were able to connect meaningfully to one another and to curricular content. She implemented the journals with a kindergarten class and their families and continued the journals when she looped up (moved) to 1st grade with her class of dynamic, insightful, critically minded kindergartners. Some of their homes were neatly sandwiched in rows of colorful trailers, with chickens clucking their way across the road, while others sat on large, tree-lined lots. Though most of the families lived below the poverty line, their lives were rich with cultural diversity, familial support, and a desire to care for their neighbors and one another. Jen's school was a

Professional Development School in partnership with our local university, which brought at least one student teacher and one practicum student to Jen's classroom every semester, along with a steady stream of university volunteers who assisted with special projects and small groups. Writing bilingual journals on a weekly or biweekly basis was possible largely because of these supports.

Elyse Schwedler, Kindergarten and 2nd-Grade Inclusion Classrooms

Elyse, a European American educator, taught 2nd grade in an urban Title 1 school with a predominantly African American and Latin@ population during her first year of journaling, and kindergarten in a rural Title 1 school with primarily European American and African American students in her second year of journaling. Elyse began using the journals to provide a meaningful platform for students to write about their learning and to connect with families. During her first year of journaling, Elyse was particularly interested in how the journals would unfold in her highly mobile, inclusion classroom. About one-fourth of the students received special educational services, and there were several schedule changes throughout the year. Eight students consistently participated in the family-dialogue-journaling process with some combination of an interventionist, a special education paraprofessional, a special education teacher, a behavior specialist, and an intern student participating throughout the year. During her second year of journaling, Elyse was interested in how journaling with kindergarten students would compare to journaling with 2nd-grade students. Although her kindergarten roster changed slightly throughout the year, 20 students and families consistently participated in the journaling process.

Jennifer Beatty, 2nd-Grade Inclusion Classroom

Jennifer had 3 years' experience with FDJs when the study group began. She taught 2nd grade in a just-opened Title 1 school of more than 900 students located in a rapidly growing urban area. Her classroom had between 19 and 26 students throughout the year, growing in number when she became the special education inclusion classroom for her grade level in November and then declining as students moved. She came from one of the surrounding schools, where she taught 1st grade, and looped to 2nd grade with five of her students, who were zoned for the new school. Jennifer is European American; her students are predominantly African American and Latin@.

Stephanie Smith, Special Education Collaborative 3rd Grade

Stephanie had just completed her third year teaching and her second year working with Family Dialogue Journals. Because she understood the complexities that accompany social injustice and critical inquiry in an elementary school classroom, she recognized the value of providing culturally sustaining (Paris, 2012) learning opportunities for her students. Stephanie used what her class called Family Weekend Journals for 3 years in a special education collaborative 3rd-grade classroom at a Title 1 school. She began and ended the year with 17 students, although 7 students moved out and 7 moved into her class. Four to 9 students throughout the year received special services. Stephanie had a full-time collaborative special education teacher as well as a paraprofessional in her class during writing for half of the year. Stephanie is European American; her students were primarily African American and Latin@. While these demographics don't showcase the laughter, curiosity, excitement, and struggles that she and her classes experienced together, they may help you understand her classroom a bit better. Over 3 years with three classes, the same difficulties arose. However, each year she felt that the benefits outweighed the challenges, which she discusses later in the book.

Joseph Jones, Middle School Graduation Coach

A graduation coach provides support to students who have been identified as at risk for dropping out of school, as forecast by predictors including previous retentions, standardized math and reading scores, math and reading grades, excessive school absences, discipline referrals, and socioeconomic status. Joseph, an African American educator, served as counselor, tutor, academic coach, social worker, mentor, community liaison, and sometimes "translator" between students and parents. He implemented FDJs with one group of 18 of his 60 students, mostly 8th-graders. Joseph described them as "first-generation English-speakers, first-generation American citizens, first-generation high school graduates and college matriculants. These are my children. If only I can wedge myself into the routine and experiences of these students, I can get them to realize all the potential they have within themselves, they will carry that into their high school experience and persist on to postsecondary educational opportunities."

Angela Dean, College Preparatory 10th-Grade Language Arts

At the time of this study, Angela was entering her ninth year of teaching. She provides a wonderful example of a short-term implementation of FDJs. Students, their families, and Angela completed ten entries, most during a literature study focusing on Nikki Grimes's novel *Bronx Masquerade*. She wanted to push students to raise critical questions about how culture is shaped, how society accepts certain cultures while rejecting others, and how the students accepted or rejected aspects of their cultural lives. The study took place within Angela's two college preparatory (the lowest of four academic tracks) sophomore language arts classes that met for 55 minutes daily. College preparatory students have mixed educational goals, interests, and motivations. Those whose needs are met by the curriculum sit next to those who feel the curriculum has little to do with their lives or future plans. Each class had 24 to 25 students, with several moving in and out between semesters, and included seniors who needed to make up credit in order to graduate. Both classes had students who had recently moved from a sheltered English language learner classroom. Each classroom had students with Individualized Education Plans. Students came from two-parent, single-parent, and grandparent-headed homes. Angela is European American; her students represented multiple cultural groups.

Amber Simmons, Senior Advanced Placement Language and Composition

At the time of the study, Amber Simmons was a high school teacher in a middle- to upper-class suburban community. As a child, Amber experienced poverty and neglect, but when adopted by her grandparents, she enjoyed the security and privilege of the middle class. She now shares the middle-class privileges of her students and fits the social norms of the community as a European American, middle-class woman. Therefore, while she is an insider to the community as an alumna of the school at which she teaches, she has not forgotten the experiences associated with hardship and need. Amber strives to be an advocate for the disadvantaged by exposing her middle-class students to the struggles of those outside of their community and outside of their experience. Amber implemented Family Dialogue Journals in her 12th-grade AP Language and Composition class. Students had diverse ethnic backgrounds, but shared similar economic backgrounds as all lived in the surrounding community and none was eligible for free or reduced-price lunch. To Amber, students in the class seemed more unified by economic similarity than divided by ethnic differences.

JoBeth Allen, Language and Literacy Education

JoBeth was the codirector of the Red Clay Writing Project and taught courses in writing, critical pedagogies, and family–school partnerships. She provided the age, if not the wisdom, in the group. Her experience with Family Dialogue Journals began 2 decades earlier when she studied with 1st- and 2nd-grade teachers Betty Shockley and Barbara Michalove (Shockley, Michalove, & Allen, 1995) as they created relationships through Family Reading Journals.

Table 1.1. Family Dialogue Journal Teachers and Students

Teacher	Grade/ Subject Using FDJs	Teaching Experience	Teacher Ethnicity	School Demographics (Rounded)
Jen McCreight	1st grade	8 years	European American	69% Latin@ 24% African American 7% European American 99% FRL*
Elyse Schwedler	2nd grade special education inclusion	3 years	European American	2% Asian 71% African American 20% Latin@ 3% European American 4% Multiracial 98% FRL
	kindergarten	1 year		1% Asian 25% African American 11% Latin@ 1% Native American 61% European American 2% Multiracial 70% FRL
Jennifer Beaty	2nd grade special education inclusion	10 years	European American	5% Asian 47% African American 41% Latin@ 3% Multiracial 3% European American 89% FRL
Stephanie Smith Mathews	3rd grade special education and ESL collaborative classrooms	3 years	European American	55% African American 40% Latin@ 1% Multiracial 3% European American 96% FRL
Joseph Jones	6th–8th grade graduation coach and 8th grade Language Arts	4 years	African American	54% African American 35% Latin@ 8% European American 3% Multiracial 94% FRL
Angela Dean	10th grade college prep World Literature	9 years	European American	0.3% Indian 11% Asian 20% Latin@ 21% African American 43% European American 5% Multiracial 26% FRL
Amber M. Simmons	12th Advance Placement Language and Composition	8 years	European American	7% Latin@ 60% European American 16% African American 14% Asian 22% FRL

*Receiving free or reduced-price lunch

CHAPTER 2

Getting Started

Focusing on Learning, Dialogue, and Relationships

We implemented Family Dialogue Journals for one compelling purpose: to connect what our students learned at school and at home. We hoped FDJs would be a two-way bridge that would allow us to bring what we learned from families into our curriculum and for families to be actively involved in what students learned in school. But like the best of educational practices, each of us also identified individual purposes for the implementation of FDJs.

MULTIPLE AND EVOLVING PURPOSES

Jennifer wanted her students and their families to discuss what was going on at school and how it connected to their home life. She envisioned this happening, not only through writing, but also in conversations at home that expanded upon the students' work together and touched on family connections, family history, family culture, and seeing the world through a critical lens. Through sharing students' and families' entries, Jennifer believed she and her students would gain insight into their extended classroom community in terms of family values, culture, opinions, memories, and academic connections.

Stephanie's purpose stemmed from a childhood experience with writing. While Stephanie now journals and finds great calm in doing so, as an elementary student she felt annoyed and irritated when she was asked to journal daily. She remembers thinking, *nothing has happened since yesterday for me to write about.* Even more, her teacher was going to read what she wrote, which meant she could not disclose personal feelings about the never-ending homework assignments or her new crush's name. Stephanie did not want her students to feel the same anxiety, especially since many of them struggled with putting words on paper. She wanted FDJs to be enjoyable for everyone, including family members. As she thought about her adverse reaction to the term *journal*, she reflected upon her own goals and desires for this project. In addition to wanting the journals to engage students, families, and teachers in meaningful dialogue that encouraged trust and open communication, Stephanie wanted to provide authentic writing opportunities that resulted in more-fluent writing.

At the secondary level, Angela's purpose initially stemmed from her concern about her students' ability and willingness to reflect deeply on issues of cultural identity. While they often had lively discussions of literature, such as *Bronx Masquerade* (Grimes, 2002), Angela wanted to push students to raise critical questions about how people shape culture, how society accepts certain cultures while rejecting others, and how the students accepted or rejected aspects of their cultural lives. After her students shared multimedia projects based on George Ella Lyons's poem "Where I'm From" (1999), Angela noticed that while some students critically examined their identity, culture, and society, others struggled to find aspects of their cultural lives they deemed worthy of sharing. Angela hoped that students would use FDJs to write with their families about issues of culture that were central to the literature they were reading.

Angela's second reason for incorporating the Family Dialogue Journals was to encourage parent and guardian participation in student learning. Based on her experience, by 10th grade most of her college-preparatory (a lower track than honors and Advanced Placement) students' parents seemed less involved in events like the school's open house and parent–teacher conferences. In the past, Angela had primarily contacted parents and guardians about negative performance or behavior through phone calls, emails, or SST (student support team) conferences. Often the parent talked of feeling at a loss as to what to do with their child and how to motivate him or her to meet the demands of school. If the students were present, they sometimes spoke on their own behalf; more often, they slumped their shoulders and cast their eyes downward. It was excruciating for Angela to witness student after student try to disappear into the paisley-print of the overstuffed conference chairs. Faculty seemed to have few strategies other than directing families to purchase an agenda book to help the child keep track of her or his assignments and to become more responsible. Wanting to find ways of bringing the families into the classroom in a positive way, Angela decided to try the Family Dialogue Journals. She hoped that by valuing family funds of knowledge, she would begin to shift the relationships she had with families and students. She wanted her role regarding the journals to be not an evaluator but rather a learner who explored the questions honestly and openly as she hoped her students and families might.

Across town and with her 12th-grade Advanced Placement students, Amber also saw FDJs as a place for students, parents, and teachers to dialogue about literature and how it related to the human experience. She invited families to offer their perspectives and insights regarding the literature and questions posed by the teacher and students, while also posing questions themselves. She did not use the journal to communicate due dates or to give updates on students' performance or behavior, which would have destroyed the sanctity of the dialogue. Amber did not want students to see the journal as a threat to their relationship with their parents, but as an opportunity to include their families in the engaging discussions they experienced in class.

As an Advanced Placement teacher, Amber was bound by the College Board standards and had to make sure that FDJs fit into the approved curriculum for AP Language and Composition. AP classes are test driven—students, administration, and other stakeholders are extremely concerned about students' AP exam scores; therefore, the test often drives the AP curriculum. The journals provided a unique, extended opportunity for talking and writing about texts that students would be required to discuss when taking the AP exam. Amber reasoned that incorporating families into their discussion encouraged students to read critically, develop clear arguments, consider multiple perspectives, and add to their depth of knowledge.

Although Amber's original purpose was to increase family engagement in the academic lives of her students and include students' home experiences in the classroom, as the year developed, the purpose of the Family Dialogue Journals progressed into something even more meaningful. While students shared personal experiences with racial stereotyping and gender bias, few appeared to have experienced financial or societal hardship. Students rarely questioned the dominant ideology that privileged their particular culture and values or the stereotypes of people affected by poverty. In class discussions, they seemed unwilling or unable to see the various factors that may have contributed to their poverty. Therefore, Amber expanded her goal of promoting three-way academic discussions to incorporate a critical perspective by including writing prompts that encouraged her students to question their ideology while also engaging their parents in these topics. She hoped that through such dialogue her students would become more socially active and critically aware citizens.

MULTIPLE TEACHER ROLES

Teachers are facilitators and participants in the family dialogue journaling process. However, based on the purposes teachers identify, they adapt the journaling process to best serve their students and families. Our experiences illustrate that processes may evolve, not only from one year to the next, but also within the year. We did keep in mind that the journals should remain a low-risk form of writing and a comfortable place to express and explore ideas. Beyond that, we tried to be reflective in the process and to try variations when something wasn't working. Most importantly, we focused on enjoyment and learning with students and families.

Introducing Journals to Students and Families

One of our first steps was to select the writing journals that fit our needs. Spiral notebooks, composition books, and three-ring binders all work well. We considered our students' abilities and needs and the content area(s) in which the journal was used. A three-ring binder made sense when students were gathering artifacts from home and/or school. For example, when our journaling topic centered on a poem from class, we included a copy of the poem in the journal. A three-ring binder also allowed for journaling emails to be printed and stored in Angela's classes. A spiral notebook was more appropriate for students who had mastered the mechanics of writing and need something more portable. Composition books have a durable cover, making them less susceptible to damaging spills or tears that might compromise the entries inside. Some students corresponded with someone who did not live in their primary residence, so they used email or letters. We learned that it was wise to store extras for the surprises that each school year holds, such as changes in class rosters or the bullmastiff who thinks the journal is a chew toy.

In her first year of journaling, Elyse purchased inexpensive composition books with sewn pages at the back-to-school sales. The wide-lined pages allowed her 2nd-grade students to format their own letters. In her second year of journaling, she chose three-prong folders for her kindergartners. The folders were lightweight and portable while allowing her to put different kinds of writing paper in to meet the quickly evolving needs of her young students.

Next on the journal preparation to-do list was to write an introductory letter. Readers could adapt one of our introductory letters (below). We wanted our letters to express excitement for the project, summarize the process, share the purpose, and provide tips for working with children as they learn to express their ideas on paper. We included this letter in the front of each journal, either by gluing or placing it in a protective sleeve.

Written in both English and Spanish versions, Jen's letter to her first-graders' families encouraged them to focus on the conversations they had about, and connections they made to, the topic of each journal. This is Jen's letter, borrowed from colleague Andrea Neher and incorporating advice from Davis and Yang (2005):

Dear Parents,
      The children and I have an exciting new project to share with you: the Weekend Family Journal. Each Friday, your child will bring home a letter s/he wrote to you, telling one thing about that week at school. Please read each week's message and ask your child to tell you about the message and any drawing with it. Don't worry if the message is

difficult to read—it is written by your first-grader's spelling ☺ Your child's messages will become easier to read as the year progresses.

Please write a message back to your child each week in the notebook right after your child's message. Anyone at home is welcome to write back—a parent, a sibling or another relative, or a family friend. The message may be written in English, Spanish, or both languages. The important thing is that your child receives a reply. When your child brings the journal back to school, I will write a message to both you and your child that you can read together the next time the journal goes home.

To keep this project working smoothly, please

- Talk together, and then write, about the same topic as your child.
- Use print, not cursive, writing.
- Have your child read your message over with you.
- Send the journal back with your child each Monday. Your child may share your message with the class.

The at-home part of this project should take no more than 10 or 15 minutes. This short routine, done each week, can be so helpful to your child's learning. Thank you for partnering with your child in this important work!

Please let me know if you have any questions.

Sincerely,
Mrs. McCreight

Amber, working with high school students, also stapled an introductory letter to the inside of their journals that explained the purpose of the project, reiterated the benefits of the project by including the results of previous research, and clearly outlined the parents' role in the dialogue (Amber assumed that parents would be the ones responding, so she addressed "Parents," while others of us wrote the more general "Families"). She wrote:

Dear Parents,

In an effort to create dialogue between students, parents, and teachers, I am assigning a dialogue journal where parents will be asked to respond to their students' writing. Studies have proven that the more often a parent reads and responds to his/her child's writing, the more quickly the student improves in thinking and writing about texts. The philosophy behind this journal is to further support students' critical thinking and writing skills through written dialogue with their parents and teachers. Not only will this reinforce the academic community we have at [school's name], but it will allow you to see the development of your child's writing and the sophistication of their thinking.

In order for this to be successful, as the student will be graded on the completion of these journals, you will be asked to do a little writing yourself. Your student will be given a prompt to which he/she will respond. As you read your student's response, I would like you to do *one* of the following:

A. Respond to something your student wrote in his/her response
B. Respond to the prompt your student wrote on
C. Respond to a question that your student poses to you in their response

The next week, you will see my response to the entry, creating a three-way dialogue. I am looking forward to us working together to support your student's writing development and critical thinking skills. I am sure that the rich dialogue produced by this journal will be memorable to both you and your student as they complete their last year in high school.

Warm Regards,
Amber Simmons

Our letters consisted of varying purposes, information, and requests depending on students' grade level and reading and writing ability. However, each of us began this process by clearly communicating our purpose, goals, and what exactly we were asking of students and family members. We emphasized what research consistently shows: when parents know that what they are doing will help their children learn and be successful in school, they are more likely to participate (Allen, 2007).

With a stack of shiny new journals ready, it was time to talk with families. The letters were not enough; most of us issued personal invitations by phone or in person. Building students' and families' excitement and understanding of the journaling process and purpose was key to our preparation. Setting a strong foundation where students and families understand the logistics of the project allowed more focus to be on the written dialogue. Creating an understanding that the family discussions and writing in the journals support student learning seemed to pave the way for a more meaningful and enjoyable journaling experience.

Elyse shared her excitement and explained Family Dialogue Journals at a Meet Your Teacher event. She showed families the journals and explained a little about the process and purpose. Meet Your Teacher events can be overwhelming, with a surplus of information, so she provided a Welcome to Second Grade newsletter in English and Spanish summarizing all the classroom information. She then called every parent in the first 2 weeks of school to welcome them to 2nd grade, invite them to the open house, and reiterate the special activities happening in their classroom—including the Family Dialogue Journals. By the time she led the first journaling workshop, she had spoken with at least one family member from each student's life either in person or on the phone.

Introducing Journals to Administrators

By sharing the goals and purposes of the FDJ project with the administration, many teachers found they were more likely to get the materials and support needed to ensure its success. Below is an example of a letter Amber submitted to her principal:

> Dear [Principal],
>
> I am currently utilizing Family Dialogue Journals in my classroom to create connections with our students' families. The focus in the journals is on how parents or caregivers and we as teachers can collaborate to support student learning. The Family Dialogue Journals, which I will be sending home after the completion of our first major novel, focus on what students are learning with me. Students write in the journals and ask their parents a question related to what they are learning; a family member writes back, and I respond to them in the journal. Research has shown that such ongoing communication is one of the most effective forms of parental involvement because families can do it at home and because it focuses on academics.
>
> Please let me know if you have any questions or suggestions regarding this engaging project. I hope you see this project as a good fit for our school's improvement goals related to family engagement, cultural competence, and academic achievement. Furthermore, I would like to make the journals available to you as artifacts of student–parent–teacher correspondence in our school as we continue to lead the county in the use of culturally engaging and inclusive teaching and communication methods.
>
> Sincerely,
> Amber Simmons

Instead of crafting a letter, Jen met with her principal to discuss the journals. She explained FDJs and their focus on building family–school partnerships, as well as the promise they held in encouraging students to write authentically about what they learned in school, thus increasing the children's likelihood of finding these topics to be relevant and worthy of re- membering. Jen's principal enthusiastically supported the idea, understand- ing she would regularly see Jen's students engaged in the journal process during Writing Workshop time. This initial conversation and consensus building later led to her principal's support of Jen's Family Writing Workshop Night at the school, thus promoting a culture of partnership beyond the Family Dialogue Journals.

Our willingness to share successful methods with our professional community encouraged further collaboration and fostered cooperation. As a result, our administrators supported family engagement in student learning.

Scheduling and Facilitating FDJ Use

Each of us had to figure out how to manage the implementation of the journals, taking time to consider our class and school calendar, the best day to write home, and how long each journaling cycle should take. With a schedule set, we tried to maintain a clear process while recognizing when we needed to address situations or make changes as schedules were altered or student motivation either increased or decreased.

It was helpful to include our students in the problem-solving process. When Jen and her students looped from kindergarten to 1st grade, their desire to write lengthier journal entries eventually caused frustration, as they had only 45 minutes available for writing. Some students were unable to finish each week, so they discussed solutions and collectively settled on a biweekly schedule according to which each writing session would last twice as long as it originally had. They were then able to spend extra time on other subjects every other week. They enjoyed these concentrated, intense blocks of writing, which allowed time for other writing projects and prevented weekly aggravation and burnout.

Stephanie came to the realistic conclusion that some weeks were just not going to be as stimulating as others, and if there wasn't anything to write about, they would not force a journal entry. This reflected her strong feelings regarding the purposeful nature of this project, and her belief that it would only work if she and her students did not adhere to a rigid weekly schedule. Stephanie took her cues from the students, and there were some weeks when they did not send journals home. She found this lengthened their interest, and added to the authenticity of the journals.

Also interested in ensuring the longevity and authenticity of Family Dialogue Journals, Elyse met with her 2nd-grade class to discuss possible solutions when she noticed they were turning in fewer journals each week. One student proposed they write on a 2-week cycle. Another student thought they needed a more concrete return schedule. The class agreed that they should all turn in the journals by Wednesday each week, as opposed to allowing journals to trail in all the way to Friday morning. A structured deadline was a simple solution that put their weekly routine back on track.

Engaging Students in Journals

For each teacher, engaging students in the Family Dialogue Journal process was a unique endeavor, dependent on students' ages, backgrounds, and family structure. As a graduation coach focusing on student retention, Joseph's teaching environment was quite distinct. He saw most students only once a week. After inviting his students to participate, Joseph provided them and their families with letters of introduction and a schedule. He structured discussion around the journals much like a club meeting or corporate team-building retreat. Each began with an icebreaker and snacks. This was an important part of engaging students, as some students showed disappointment that they were missing time with friends in other classes. Joseph felt supported by his assistant principal, who helped him to explain the FDJs to families, but he knew the students needed to buy in as well.

Jen introduced her students to FDJs by reading and discussing an excerpt from the book *Home* (Rosen, 1992). In it, a conversation among family members takes place around "Grandma's kitchen table," and Jen used this to spark students' memories of where their families spent time together. Jen asked the students if they would like to invite their families to write with them throughout the school year, explaining they would agree on one topic each week to write home about. They would talk with their families about what they were learning, as written in the journal, and about the question they posed; one or more family members would write a response in the journal. Then, they would share family responses during Morning Meeting the following week. After their enthusiastic endorsement, the class decided their first entry would be about the special places their families gathered. Jen modeled by drawing a picture of herself and her husband reading on the couch, surrounded by their three dogs. The children spread out around the room to draw pictures and write words representing their own special places. As they wrote, Jen, her bilingual coteacher, and her student teacher walked around and wrote the journal's discussion question on the same page. They wrote in either Spanish or English, depending on each family's home language: *¿Dónde usted comparte historias de la familia?/Where do you share family stories?*

Jennifer used Family Dialogue Journals for multiple years, and learned the hard way that taking time to teach about FDJs upfront was critical. Her second year of implementation, she introduced them to her 1st-graders in a way that went something like this: "Okay guys we're going to do something new today! Family Journals! Yay! Let's make a list of all the things we learned this week and write a letter to our families about it, then take it home and have them write back! Okay, go!" Her third year she taught 2nd grade and, unfortunately, her introduction to the families and students was very similar. While she and her students learned a lot from the journals and they were meaningful to them as a classroom community, she thinks if she had invested time introducing them more thoroughly, they would have heard from a greater quantity of family members, as well as plunged deeper into critical issues to expand their thinking.

From her experience, Jennifer recommends the following:

- Introducing Family Dialogue Journals to the students the first week of school, as they're talking about themselves and their families, and letting them know they'll start FDJs the next week
- Introducing FDJs and their purpose to the families at open house
- Calling any families who were unable to attend open house and introducing FDJs and their purpose
- Discussing FDJ progress during home visits
- Discussing FDJ progress again at fall parent–teacher conferences

Responding to Entries

Another role of the teacher is to be what Amber calls a "genuine participant in the dialogue, listening and willing to change and adapt to the knowledge and interests that families are bringing into the classroom" (Simmons, 2013, p. 93). In the journaling process, we asked students and families to share personal details about their lives, experiences, and opinions. It would not be a true dialogue if we were not willing to do the same, and therefore, the openness of the teacher in her responses was integral to the implementation of FDJs. For example, in response to a prompt about regret, a parent of one of Amber's students wrote a personal and moving response about the guilt she felt about rushing to get off the phone with her mother only to find out that her mother had passed away later that day. The parent stated, "It changed my life at that moment, and it changed my life forever. I always regret that I did not take the time to talk to her as long as she had wanted to. My mind keeps echoing the thought 'I wish I had spoken to her longer.'" When receiving such an intimate and obviously emotional response, it would be inappropriate for the teacher to respond with a curt "thanks for sharing" or trite "that's so sad." Instead, Amber wrote, "[My grandmother] repeats stories. I want to cut her short, so I often snap at her saying that I've heard that story a million times . . . Your story has reminded me to enjoy the sound of her voice, even if I've already heard the story, because she won't be around forever." In this case, Amber reciprocated with details about her own life and pointed out the valuable lesson she gained from the parent's experience.

Elyse also found that sharing personal thoughts through her 2nd-grade journals was a vulnerable experience. Elyse tried to be honest and genuine without dominating the conversation, but sometimes she struggled with the idea of being vulnerable. In February, her class decided to write home about Jackie Robinson and formed the question, "Who has been a role model in your life?" The following week, Malcom raised his hand to share his father's response during morning meeting.

> Malcom your grandmother was a big role model to me cause, she raise me by herself. She made everyday special in some way. She showed me how to be a man by inplanting the love for people in my heart. That is why i try to help everyone i can. That's why i have you with me cause i wasn't going to stand by and let you be hurt 1 more day. And i just want to let you no that i love you very much and i promise to fight hard again to keep you with me!

Knowing some of the students' difficult history, Elyse's eyes filled with tears. Malcom closed his journal, looked up nonchalantly and said, "Ummmmm . . . are you going to cry?" Elyse smiled and said that she was so happy he had a dad who loved him so much. Malcom grinned, put his journal on the table, and headed back to his seat without saying another word. Elyse did not say another word either, until she sat down to respond. This parent had been so honest—so loving. She felt she was intruding on a father's personal letter and declaration to his son, and she did not know how or if she should respond.

She considered possible responses, such as making a connection to her relationship with her grandmother or telling about her own role models. Malcom's father had a passionate message for his son that moved her tremendously but did not involve her, so she decided to address Malcom as well.

> There are many people who love you and want you to be successful. I know you have some wonderful role models in your life. I don't know much about your grandmother, but she sounds wonderful too! Please know that I am here if you (or your family) ever need something I can help with!

Sometimes it can be difficult to find the appropriate words. Elyse worried, "Should I have spent more time selecting my words to show I cared?" Nevertheless, conversations in person and on the phone that followed let her know Malcom and his family had warmly received her message.

Similarly, Jennifer found that navigating the roles of family, student, and teacher could be complex. She had a hard time figuring out how she fit in because she was trying to respond to both the families and students every week. Sometimes her questions went unanswered, for example, "What are some of the strategies you learned? Kiki, are some of your mom's strategies the same as what we're learning?" and "That sounds great! Do you still make any of those treats with pumpkins?" Jennifer felt these questions lacked authenticity, and that her voice was superfluous to the intimate conversation taking place between students and families. She tried to find the purpose of her voice through talking with her study group. Jennifer realized that the written dialogue between student and family was much more important than anything she could say, but she decided to continue writing something—anything—so the students and families knew she was reading and reflecting on their dialogue. Sometimes she wrote a personal connection, such as when she responded to an entry about a family event by saying:

> My family likes to help people too. There's always a person in my mom's life that she visits and runs errands for—usually a woman who she somehow meets that's having a hard time. I think having her as a role model growing up made me want to help others, too.

Other times she wrote generally about the student:

> Thank you all for sharing! I've really enjoyed being Jocelyne's teacher for the last 2 years! She's very sweet, thoughtful, talented, smart, and driven to do her best. I will miss you all!

Jennifer felt most gratified when her families or students responded to what she wrote, such as this dialogue with Maria's mother. In one such exchange, Jennifer asked,

> Dear Maria and mom,
>   Where in Mexico did you live? Maria have you been to Mexico? Do you still have family there?

Maria's mom responded,

> We live in Michoacán, Mexico. Maria hasn't been to Mexico, but she is anxious to go. Yes, we still have a lot of family there in Mexico.

Jennifer wanted the students and their families to know that she was as committed to the journals as they were, even though she didn't always know how to respond.

In her high school English classroom, Angela found that family responses sometimes provided models that students could use to produce entries rich in detail and dialogic possibility. Therefore, she developed a way to use some of them, along with questioning techniques and rereading, in an early exploration of how to write in this way. She introduced the Family Dialogue Journals to her students in November around Thanksgiving break. Students were traveling to see family and friends and Angela hoped it would be a time when they could collect their first entries, possibly from family members who would not always be able to participate. She glued a letter to participants and two possible prompts into the composition books:

What is a tradition you value most in your family? Describe that tradition and what takes place. Who is present? Why is it special to you individually and/or to your family as a whole?

Or

What is a tradition you'd like to have in your family when you become an adult? Describe this tradition and explain when it would take place. Who would be present? Why is this something that you'd like for your family to take part of?

Garrett wrote:

The tradition that I value the most in my family is waking up at 5 o'clock in the morning to sneak down stairs on Christmas morning to see my presents. My siblings are present with me every Christmas, but this Christmas it won't happen. Some of the reasons are 1. I won't have my entire family with me there to do it and 2. I will be in Texas visiting my family. Why is it special? It is special because we get children bonding time and the parents don't know about it.

Garrett's father wrote:

In the corner sits the tree, tall decorated and illuminated with colored lights surrounded by brightly colored wrapped packages, taunting children as time passes. The morning breaks and Santa has come and gone leaving gifts for all; thoughts of lumps of coal creep into the back of the minds of the children slyly sneaking downstairs. Stockings stuffed and gifts separated by child, as only Santa can do, fill the room as the excitement builds and the wide-eyed looks absorb just what has been left behind by the jolly old elf. Parents are content knowing all will be excited and happy when all surprises can be had.
    Memories of time passed; thoughts of how this Christmas will be different. The conflicting thoughts cancel each other as reality breaks upon the mind . . . shuddering at the thought of being at the in-laws, the possibility of not being together as a family again all weigh on the mind. Traditions of a family change as time passes and situations change. Hopefully this tradition will not be cast aside as time passes. The future is uncertain, just as the present is tenuous.

Garrett's father's beautifully detailed entry got Angela thinking about how families' responses might be used as models in the classroom. She noticed that oftentimes families provided a lot of descriptive detail, but the student might not. Angela also noticed that there were a few journals through which both family and child might be able to develop further in their descriptive writing. In journals where Angela wanted more development, either from the child, the parent, or both, she posed questions for the student. She wanted to create a culture with the FDJs where writing with rich description and thoughtful details was the norm.

Therefore, in response to Garrett and his father, Angela wrote the following:

> Wow! Such descriptive details. It is tough to balance it all and hard to have to shift the way we've always done things. My parents have moved from the town where I grew up and for the past 2 years we've celebrated Christmas at their new home and not in Newnan. It has been a strange transition and I'm not sure how I feel about it yet. Garrett, what sort of fun things do you and your cousins, brothers, sisters get into? I'd love to hear about the trip to Texas and new things you all do. I'd also love to hear about ways you bring those who can't physically be there into the day(s) you celebrate.

Angela passed back the journals and gave the students time to develop an entry where they addressed her questions. Garrett replied:

> The fun things that me and my cousins and siblings like to do on Christmas Eve is to play fun things outside. Back in Texas, I was a big-time hockey player and we got a trampoline so me and my older brother would have a tournament of Trampoline Hockey. Then on New Year's Eve we played a tournament of ultimate frisbee. This was fun because we are all so athletic and competitive that it helps us to determine who has power in the house and who controls the remote (currently Karee does that, but that will change). Then we come inside and drink hot chocolate and watch TV with my sister. I love do this and I hope I can do it all again.

Many students, like Garrett, focused on Christmas day or Thanksgiving, building details into their writing because of Angela's probing. Camilla, however, focused on a tradition that leads up to the celebration of Christmas in her family. She wrote:

> The tradition I value most with my family is called "Novena." Every year my whole family which includes my parents, brother, cousins, aunts, uncles, grand-parents, family friends and I start the Novena. The Novena is a series of prayers lasting 9 days, which begin on December 16 'til the 24th of December. During the Novenas everyone sings songs and celebrates the three Kings' journey to meet baby Jesus. After we have FOOD! The best part ☺. Doing the Novenas is

special to me because I like the feeling of being united with all of my family and having food, singing and laughing with everyone. I believe everyone cherishes those special moments during Christmas time.
Do you cherish every moment of the Novena as much as I do?

Camilla's mother responded:

Yes I do, because the "Novena" is a tradition that I have followed all my life and I'm glad that I have now passed it on to you and I hope you pass it on to your children. Praying the Novena in our family signifies the true meaning of Christmas.

In response to Camilla and her mother, Angela wrote:

This sounds like a wonderful family tradition. I'd love to hear more about the songs and the food ☺! Thank you for sharing this with me.

Camilla responded to Angela's entry with the following:

Mrs. Dean! The songs are in Spanish, I don't think you'd understand unless you translate it. Haha! They are mainly about baby Jesus being born, and the journey to go see him on Christmas day. The food that we eat is all Colombian food like bunelos, natilla, arroz con leche, pan de queso, and sometimes empanadas. It is all really good and I'd like for you to try it one day!

The first swap was the only time Angela had students read back over what she wrote and to respond to the specific questions she raised. Across both classes, students tended to give generic descriptions and Angela wanted them to develop rich, descriptive responses. She found that taking the time to have students go back and consider further questions helped to develop a norm through the rest of the year.

STUDENT ROLES

Student talk about their learning-generated journal topics and questions. Students were responsible for communicating their learning and the class question to their families through writing and/or drawing. Their journal entries were the catalyst of written and oral responses from home and school, as they transported the journals to and from each person in the conversation. Students were the heart—and legs—of the dialogue journals.
We worked hard throughout the year to help students create prompts and questions for their parents that did not elicit a yes or no answer.

Furthermore, the prompt needed to be specific enough to relate to the content that they were studying but broad enough to provide family members who were not familiar with the specific text or content with an opportunity to respond based on their own knowledge and experiences. In addition, the student's response often served as a mentoring text for the parent, as they assumed the student understood what was required in the assignment and emulated the style and effort put forth by the student. Therefore, especially in the upper grades, the length and content of the parent's response was often comparable to the length and breadth of the student's. For instance, in Amber's journals, the parent's response was the same length as the student's response 58% of the time.

Furthermore, to develop a sense of community and to provide an opportunity to learn from students' experiences and those of their families, we asked students to share what was written in their journals (see Chapter 5). While voluntary, the practice of sharing allowed students to share their own thoughts about the topic and how it related to that of their families. Students also made cross-family connections, sometimes relating to a member of another student's family's response.

FAMILY ROLES

Families began each cycle as the audience. This gave students the authentic experience of writing to another person to inform, persuade, entertain, and gather information. The family members, both in oral and written dialogue, validated the importance and purpose of their child's written words, and they contributed to bridging learning between home and school. The journals gave families a springboard to discuss school learning and to connect home learning. Schools were then able to learn from families' experiences, opinions, and knowledge base. It is important to note that we encouraged family members to respond in their home language, and when students were unable to translate, we identified supportive educators or community members; sometimes, especially for languages less common in the United States like Tagalog, we enlisted the rough help of Google Translate to both read and respond to these entries.

Students in all our classrooms asked various members of their family and community to contribute to their FDJ. For example, in Amber's classroom, when Beth's brother was home from college for the weekend, he wrote in the journal. Josh, a student who lived with his mother and grandparents, oftentimes had his grandmother respond when his mother was not available. Mandy, who usually had her father respond to the journal, asked her neighbor to write in it when she visited one day. Because the journals address the family, not just parents, students felt that they could ask anyone who knew them well to respond to the journal.

NECESSARY SUPPORT STRUCTURES

Implementation of Family Dialogue Journals was not without struggles. Many of our study group's conversations revolved around troubleshooting difficulties. The resolutions to these issues often came back to the importance of identifying support structures to ensure the journals' success.

Time

As is often the case, teachers sometimes struggled to find the time to implement Family Dialogue Journals. With other projects to complete and standards to cover, as well as scheduling interruptions like school assemblies or classroom guidance sessions, it took resolve, perseverance, and creative thinking to maintain some semblance of regularity in completing the journals, sending them home, and carving out time for sharing responses the following week.

In Jen's classroom, she dedicated her Morning Meeting sharing time to discussion of FDJs. Each morning, four students read their journal entry and their family's response and would then call on two classmates to ask questions and comment on the information they shared. This structure allowed all students to share by week's end, empowered the children to create the dialogue surrounding their FDJs, and ensured the time would not drag on beyond what their 6-year-old attention spans could handle. Though Jen limited the time spent in dialogue during this sharing circle, she often heard the children engaging in conversation about journal responses while at lunch or on the playground, letting her know they were learning from and with one another beyond Morning Meeting.

Translators

Many students' families spoke languages other than English in their homes, so translating journal entries from home to school and back again was an incredibly important logistical detail each teacher considered. Some students translated for their families, some enlisted older siblings to translate, and some schools offered translation services to teachers and families. No one approach worked for everyone, as participants and resources were individual to each classroom.

Elyse used an online translator when parents wrote in Spanish, while Jen enlisted the help of her coteacher, a native Honduran, in this task. He graciously translated the children's question to their families, the family responses as students returned them the following week, and Jen's response back to each family. In Stephanie's class, the students whose families responded in Spanish also knew how to read Spanish and translate these responses themselves. This made sharing fun because they would read it in

Spanish and then give the English translation. Some schools enlisted bilingual family engagement specialists to aid in translation.

Amber had one student who came to her after class and told her that his parents spoke Urdu, a language found mostly in Pakistan and India, and did not write English very well. He said that he asked his mother the question and then wrote down what she said. Allowing a student to translate for a parent required a degree of trust that they were not fabricating the parent's response. Therefore, Amber asked how he implemented his parent "interview" at home. He said that he asked his mother the question at dinner and wrote down her response and that being able to talk with her allowed her to ask questions about the prompt, his own response to the prompt, and the curriculum to which the question referred. He said that he summarized her thoughts on the topic as they discussed the question. Amber was pleased that the student and his mother participated in extended verbal dialogue about the question, which was the goal of the FDJ in the first place.

Support Teachers and Community Members

Support teachers and community members were incredibly important to the success of Family Dialogue Journals, and they contributed in unique ways. For instance, Stephanie taught in a collaborative classroom. During Writer's Workshop a special education collaborative teacher assisted students with writing challenges. In the middle of the year, there was an influx of students with writing and behavior difficulties; in response, the school hired a paraprofessional. Students formed groups based on who was writing about a similar topic or asking the same question that week. With so many adults in the room, groups were always flexible and teachers often rotated among students.

In Jen's classroom, a few families did not regularly respond to the journals. Jen and the students in this situation talked about how the journals were not the only way for everyone to learn about and share information with families and that they would continue to communicate in many ways. The students then decided a community member who volunteered in their room every week could respond to their journals when families could not. The volunteer ensured that every child contributed to and felt part of the classroom dialogue around FDJs. Family members were still encouraged and given the opportunity to answer each week, but Jen felt much more secure in the process when she knew every student was guaranteed a response.

"This is all very interesting," you might be saying, "but exactly what do I write? What do the students write? I've got the big picture, so now I'm ready to start having those conversations with my students and generating questions." You are in luck. Chapter 3 is all about generating those journal entries.

Mini-Lesson Idea: Why Are We Writing Home?

Prior to This Lesson

- Read *Dear Mrs. LaRue: Letters from Obedience School* by Mark Teague with younger students, or a section from another book in letter format with older students.
- Create a tree map entitled "Reasons to Write" in the classroom to be added to and referenced during the lesson and as needed thereafter.
- Post 4 to 6 posters around the classroom for students to rotate to, such as . . .
  - » Why might you create a letter or email?
  - » Why might you create a poster?
  - » Why might you create a list?
  - » How do you use writing in your daily life?

Opening

Show several forms of writing (journals, posters, books, lists, recipes) and explain that there are many reasons to write. Connect to Family Dialogue Journals by explaining that "we will write home to tell our families about what we have learned and to learn from our families."

Mini-Lesson

1. Review *Dear Mrs. LaRue: Letters from Obedience School* by reading a letter or two and asking students to share why they think Ike is writing home.
2. After students have shared ideas, introduce the tree map, "Reasons to Write," and add Ike's reason to write—to persuade.
3. Explain that we will consider our own reasons to write today. Students meet in groups (depending on the number of posters). Groups write their responses to each poster's question directly onto the poster using markers. Each group spends 1 to 2 minutes discussing and responding to each poster and then rotates to the next poster.
4. After students have discussed and responded to each poster, each group shares the class's ideas by orally sharing the last poster they responded to.

Student Work

Students write letters home in their journals about the reasons they write, making sure to ask families the question, "What are your reasons for writing?"

Closing

Review reasons for writing by referring back to the "Reasons to Write" tree map and add ideas generated from the poster activity and related discussion.

CHAPTER 3

Generating Journal Entries

Questions are what make the Family Dialogue Journals dialogic. We worked with our students to pose authentic questions to families, questions that would generate meaningful conversations at home, deepen our understanding of what we were studying, and bring family voices into the curriculum.

GENERATING LETTERS AND QUESTIONS

The journaling process unfolded uniquely in each classroom. Generating journal entries and questions requires a collaboration of teachers and students, especially as students were learning the journaling process and developing this genre of writing. Our weekly or biweekly FDJ workshops followed a similar format. The workshop began with a discussion of the week's learning. "What have we learned this week that has been most interesting? What stands out the most when you think back on (various learning experiences across) the week? What do you think your families would want to know about? What could you teach your family?" We found this regular, anticipated "week in review" not only led us to topics for the FDJs, it gave us insights into what students found interesting, valuable, and memorable about their learning that week. For example, in Stephanie's 3rd-grade class each week, children piled around on the rug or in chairs and "buddy chatted" about favorite book titles, fun science experiments, visitors, or new playground games. Stephanie then opened the floor for the students to share ideas to include in their FDJ letters. She recorded this list on the board, and students then brainstormed their burning question for family members to respond to.

In Elyse's 2nd grade, she modeled how to use the classroom environment to help generate ideas. She prompted students to look at the posted Essential Questions (required by the school, these are open-ended "big idea" questions), the "What's up in math?" bulletin board, and displayed student work. Her class generated three to five ideas that she recorded on a "What did we learn this week?" circle map. For example, one week the chart included (1) modeling numbers, (2) *Tacky the Penguin* (Lester, 1990), and (3) taking a test on the computer. Elyse had to consciously avoid stating her opinion in order to allow students to guide the topic selection and subsequent class vote. Although she was hoping to continue the conversation sparked by the reading of *Tacky the Penguin* about fitting in, her students voted to write home about the benchmark tests they had taken in the computer lab. Elyse's class then created a new circle map with the blank center surrounded by students' ideas. Students shared how they felt when they took the test and the purpose of the tests. They filled the web with words and phrases, such as "nervous," "confidence," and "to show what you know." Next, the class pondered what to ask families about taking tests. The students decided on the question, "Have you ever taken a test on the computer? How did you feel?" which became the center of the web.

Throughout the year, we integrated mini-lessons on how to form questions and the importance of considering what types of responses a question will elicit. We helped students generate questions that prompted more than a yes or no response, questions that invited families to share their knowledge, feelings, and experiences. Periodically we reflected with the students on questions and responses for previous weeks: Why did our question lead to particularly long or short, rich or skimpy family responses? How can we word this question to learn more from our families?

Supporting Productive Discussions

When Jennifer taught 1st grade, she learned a valuable lesson about posing questions. Initially, she and the students generated the letter about what they learned collaboratively, she wrote it on a chart, and the students copied it in their journals. Jennifer then asked each student to write his or her own question. She was disappointed in the quality of the questions and the number of families who responded in the journal. So the next year Jennifer and her students wrote the questions together as part of their letter. She found that not only did they collectively create richer questions, but this part of the discussion often gave her the chance to clarify misconceptions and to prompt students to think critically. Because the questions were more carefully crafted (e.g., avoiding yes or no questions), responses improved significantly. The conversations around the journal entries became prime instructional time.

Joseph, a middle school graduation coach, saw his students only once a week. He created the following schedule:

- Icebreaker: 5 min
- Topic Introduction: 5 min
- Video: 10 min
- Discussion: 20 min
- Generation of Prompt: 10 min
- Write: 10 min

For Joseph there were hot topics such as relationships with parents that ignited discussion and debate, even among the quietest young people. He noted that "prying students engaged in those topics is like trying to snatch a short rib from the jaws of a pit bull. Then there are topics that are like the most dreaded of surgeries—for both the attending physician and the patient. No one wants to make that first incision, nor be the one going under the knife."

Joseph found short videos particularly effective in generating discussion. He used Internet sites that were available through the school servers that contained videos addressing any number of pertinent topics. *Channelone.com* is the website for Channel One News, a source for breaking national news, music, sports, homework help, and games and quizzes, all with a focus on students. His intent was to show the students that education was about so much more than just showing up at school every day, passing tests, and getting "good" grades; there is a quality of life associated with increased knowledge, awareness, and participation. For example, several discussions focused on health. Channel One News had a segment on Type 2 Juvenile Diabetes featuring some high school students recounting the challenges of being a teenager having to face each day as a diabetic. First Lady Michelle Obama's *Let's Move* young people's fitness initiative was another hot topic. After viewing the videos, Joseph asked students if anything they had viewed affected them personally and what health issues had to do with school. From there the discussion progressed to family expectations, future hopes and plans, and how one's health can aid or hinder students' ability to function properly throughout the school day and even affect future career possibilities.

During this conversation period, Joseph wrote principles, quotes, or phrases the students used on the board. The class used these as prompts to summarize, clarify, and shore up understanding prior to writing. Students then wrote in their composition book, starting with a summarizing paragraph explaining the conversation that had taken place in the group, followed by a question related to the conversation that students generated by consensus. Joseph provided some guiding, prompting, or clarifying as necessary, but the question emanated from the students themselves. The impetus, regardless of the topic, was, "*What do you want to know about your family?*" Whether the topic was the necessity of grades, health, career choices, or bullying, the question was meant to elicit a response from family members.

Joseph, like all teachers, knew that students varied widely in how they interacted during discussions such as these. The teacher must have a keen sense of timing and discernment, knowing when to encourage a story from a student or redirect a conversation headed toward inappropriate private business. Joseph tried to help students who dominated discussions learn to listen to classmates. Other students needed support in learning how to make their opinions known, to gain the discussion floor. And sometimes, as Joseph learned, we teachers need to respect silence. The quietest student may carry the loudest pen.

Such was the case with Joseph's student Esperanza. Her parents had instilled in her a strong work ethic and reverence for education. Esperanza was an eager learner, but was a veritable church mouse in a small group or class discussion, even among her friends. However, when the time came to create journal entries and share those entries with the folks at home, Esperanza led the way. At Joseph's encouragement for all his Spanish-speaking students, Esperanza wrote in Spanish, her parents' language. With interesting thoughts on the prompts, and one of the few to share her entries at home and garner a written response, she was the most consistent. Joseph described Esperanza as one of those trees a teacher can completely miss among the forest of other students. Her quiet demeanor hid a rich insight and experience she desired to share, just not verbally.

Journal Entries Focused on Literature

Angela's class dialogued with their families during the reading of *Bronx Masquerade* by Nikki Grimes (2002), a young adult novel tracing the varied identities of one 11th-grade English class. Written in vignettes and poetry from the perspective of the students, the book illustrates how a group of students who assumed they had very little in common and little ability to express themselves through poetry began to see one another in different ways and become writers. Through a series of discussions about this and related texts, including persuasive essays (detailed elsewhere in this book), Angela and her students generated entries each week that would draw their families into the social issues they were addressing. Some of those questions included:

- What things are accepted in your culture that might not be accepted in another? Explain what it was like to come to this realization.
- Where do we fit in society? Where do we find we are the insiders?
- How do you feel about the ways in which the media portrays beauty? How, if any, has this affected your body image?

Amber also focused FDJ entries on literature. Initially Amber provided her AP Language and Composition students with prompts. Because her goal was to foster a critical consciousness within her students, she felt the need to model critical questioning and reflection. However, after reading about the successes that other teachers were having with class-composed prompts, she compromised by writing a prompt that introduced the context on which the question would be based and let the students choose the phrasing of the actual question. One such prompt read:

> In *As I Lay Dying*, William Faulkner depicts the hierarchies of social class in the rural south. It has once been said that "Faulkner has an unusual ability to depict poor, rural folk with grace, dignity, and poetic grandeur without whitewashing or ignoring their circumstances." Students: In this week's entry, please craft a question that relates social class issues in *As I Lay Dying* to issues of class in today's world.

When she got the journals back on Monday, she was not thrilled with the results. Some of the questions were critical and elicited a detailed response from the parent. For example, Caleb, a White, athletic boy who often related his prompts to his experience on the soccer field, asked his father, "How does Faulkner's description," which was provided in the context of the prompt, "vary from the modern description of poor people?" This provided the parent with an open-ended question that led to the critical questioning of how the poor are viewed by society. However, some students did not pose a question and others posed a question so specific to the text that parents would have difficulty responding if they had not read the book. For example, Mehal, an Indian American girl who was known for asking particularly engaging questions about authors' style, asked her mother, "How does Faulkner's use of stream-of-consciousness monologues depict the social issues? Are these still a problem now?" In this question, the parent would need to be familiar with the stream-of-consciousness writing technique and have an understanding of its use in Faulkner's work. The critical element of the question was also underwhelming. Therefore, Amber felt that her students still needed guidance, so she continued to model critical questioning by composing the prompts herself.

In fact, Amber would have continued her role as question poser if it had not been for the serendipitous timing of an independent research project. Because Amber enjoys giving her students choice and power over their reading selections and research projects, students were working with various novels, from texts by Capote, Rowling, and Dan Brown to Austen, Milton, and Hemingway. Since all of her students were reading different books, she couldn't come up with a prompt that would be relevant to everyone's research. While more out of desperation than pedagogical choice, she decided to follow in the footsteps of her dialogue journal comrades and let her students, as a group, construct the prompt for the week. The only stipulation was that it had to be a topic that everyone could relate to the book that they were reading. The collaborative construction of the prompt was a success. Kali, a quick-thinking and popular African American girl, immediately came up with the idea of relating their book to a current event, and when another student asked her, "Which event?" she suggested, "How about the current conflict in Egypt?" Everyone agreed and talked about what aspects of the Egyptian crisis could be discussed in relation to their books. Discussions on topics such as oppression, revolution, betrayal, poverty, uprising, facades, inequality, and corruption ensued.

When the students brought their journals in to share on Monday, most responses were provocative and insightful. Mehal, a romantic at heart who was reading *Pride and Prejudice* (Austen, 1813/1995) wrote, "The original name of *Pride and Prejudice* was *First Impressions* and the plot centralizes around the fact that our impressions of people can turn out to be wrong. It took 30 years for the people of Egypt to see Mubarak's true colors." Her mother focused on how the Indian people were silenced by force for generations like the Egyptians were. She wrote, "I witnessed numerous revolts and sometimes the people's voice got heard. Other times they were silenced by mobs." Zuhair, a quiet, thoughtful Indian American boy, wrote the following about *Of Mice and Men*: "George shoots Lennie in the back of the head in the same way Mubarak shot Egypt," discussing how George and Mubarak betrayed people that they were supposed to be protecting. Zuhair's father wrote about witnessing the disparity of the rich and the poor in Eqypt and how despite their poverty, the Egyptian people are kind to foreigners and very hospitable.

Amber was extremely pleased that the students chose an event and writing prompt that related to social justice. She wondered if they chose such a topic because of her critical topics in the previous prompts, or if they were genuinely interested in the events in Egypt. Allowing the students to collaboratively create the next few weeks' prompts answered Amber's questions. She found that by making the creation of prompts a collaborative activity, students brainstormed and built off one another's ideas until they came up with a question that was both pleasing to everyone and critical. For example, when reading *Othello*, one student suggested that the class write about race. Amber asked, "What about race?" The students began to brainstorm and then someone said, "Oooh, Menal has a good one! Say it, Menal, say it!" Menal whispered, "What if we write about a time where we felt our racial difference?" Everyone agreed.

In the end, Amber felt as though her choice to create the prompts for her students at the beginning of the year was beneficial in that students were able to recognize the characteristics of a critical question and get accustomed to reflecting on such topics before collectively creating their own. With her guidance and the encouragement of fellow classmates, Amber's students gradually developed the skills to pose problems and ask questions, investigating and making connections between the world and the word (Freire, 1970).

Examples of Teacher-Generated Prompts:

1. We are now in the middle of our Advertisement Project. Your goal is to find all of the persuasive and rhetorical devices, literary elements, and fallacies within the advertisement your group has chosen. Write about a time when you saw an advertisement that offended you or insulted your intelligence.

2. As we read *The Importance of Being Earnest*, we can see the societal traditions, assumptions, and norms that are being satirized—for example, the views and assumptions held by the rich about the "lower" classes; the intolerance for differences; and the ridiculous abundance of formality used among friends and the insignificant, trivial things that are valued by the higher classes. Looking at the world today, what do you think deserves satirizing? What custom, expectation, tradition, and so forth do you think is a vice or obsession within our current society?

3. After reading *As I Lay Dying*, we now have a better understanding of Addie's outlook on life. She believed that life for a woman was nothing but suffering and the "reason for living was to get ready to stay dead for a long time." While we tend to think that life was hard for women "back then," are there women in today's society who might still feel the way Addie did about life? If so, who and why?

Examples of Class-Created Prompts

1. We are currently doing an individual research project on a novel of our choosing. In order to show how this book is relevant to today's society, we have chosen to connect a theme or character from the novel to a current event. How does our book relate to the present unrest in Egypt?

2. Since we are currently focusing on language and speech, we decided to look at our own usage. What are your favorite slang, dialectal, and academic terms? Why are they your favorite? When do you use them and with whom?

3. We are currently reading *Othello*, and he is constantly made the racial "other." When were you in a situation where you felt your racial, ethnic, religious, or cultural difference?

QUESTIONS THAT ELICIT STRONG RESPONSES

Generating burning questions that elicited strong responses from families was a goal all of us worked on, sometimes much more successfully than others. There were some weeks when a great question emerged from students' morning meetings, a particularly lively class discussion ("Oh—that would be a great question to ask our parents!"), or an event such as an impending test or field trip. We couldn't always figure out which questions would engage families, but we knew successes when we saw them.

One such example happened when Stephanie invited a technology specialist to collaborate in integrating technology into their curriculum. They decided to try geocaching as a way to teach social studies standards, but also as a way to include families and communities in their study of location. Geocaching is a treasure hunt game that allows students to use GPS devices to locate and hide small treasures. Millions of people are involved in geocaching throughout the world; it is a free download for many smartphones, making it available to many of Stephanie's families. Her students were ecstatic about the idea and it quickly became the talk of every Morning Meeting. She was surprised that so many students wanted to write home about it on Friday because so many had already shared throughout the week what they had been telling their parents.

Fran, while describing his week in 3rd grade, added, "And this is the best part Miss Amy came to teach us about geocache. Geocache is little or big boxes that people hide them for other people to find. Kind of taking them to places around the world." Olivia explained geocaching to her parents and older brother in her journal:

> Geocaching is like you have to have a computer or a phone that
> has GPS or we can use Uncle Jeremy's phone and you have to go to
> geocaching.com and find where a box is because it has something in it
> then you put something in it of ours and who ever finds it has to get
> it back to us and the one we got we got to try and get it back to them.
> Ms. Amy taught us that.

The students thoroughly enjoyed teaching their parents about this new technology. Stephanie heard from many parents how excited they were to see their child so engaged and excited about learning. One wrote, "You are right. I didn't know about Geocache, thanks to you now I know . . . I would love to go to Geocache with you one day." Another parent responded, "I would like to learn more about Geocaching. It sounds interesting!" Many offered to join them on their geocaching outing. After their geocaching field trip to the local park, one student took her parents back to the park to show them the geocache that they found as a class.

Another week Stephanie had special guests observing from China and Taiwan. The students asked them to say something in their native language. The girls taught the class to say "I love you" in Chinese. That Friday, the class all agreed to teach their parents their new Chinese phrase and then ask their parents, "Do you know any words in another language?" During the spring the class became a home for six baby chicks. The whole class was enamored when they hatched, and some students wanted to write about them in their family journals. Others wanted to ask families about their science experiment about heat and insulation; they decided to ask their parents, "How would you choose to save an ice cube?" The chick advocates asked, "Did you have a class pet when you were in school?" Stephanie realized that the best responses came when the students were most engaged in their topic and that choice of topics led to increased engagement.

In Amber's classroom, questions that elicited strong responses differed for students and families. Students responded to class-generated questions with more enthusiasm and depth, which resulted in longer entries with more specific details. For a prompt about favorite words, both slang and academic, many students wrote close to three pages listing the words, explaining their meaning and why they liked them so much. Some students even wrote about words that they made up themselves, explaining how they were now a part of their identity. However, for parents, the questions about current events spurred more-detailed responses. The prompt regarding the unrest in Egypt was of particular interest to parents. It is possible that parents felt more knowledgeable about the topic since it had dominated news reports for weeks.

In addition, parents responded more strongly when their child wrote about an experience that the child had not previously shared with them. For example, Kelly, when responding to a prompt about when she felt different from others, shared some circumstances where she felt very uncomfortable (Amber agreed not to share the specifics in this book). Her mother wrote:

> It was really interesting and insightful to read about Kelly's awkward situations. I can see how she felt out of place in the situation she was in and reading it makes me feel sad because a mom always wants her child to be happy and feel at ease in every situation. I realize that this is what life is all about, and a child needs to encounter situations like these and learn for themselves how to handle them. They also get to learn that they, too, are truly special for who they are and what they believe in even if some other people are different and don't agree.

In the remaining chapters of the book we share multiple examples of journal entries that elicit strong responses, sometimes by a single parent, as in Kelly's case, and sometimes for the majority of the class. There is no formula for such elicitation. There is only engaging in the process, reflecting on it, and refining it, as we see in the next section.

EVOLVING PROCESSES DURING THE YEAR

The second Friday morning in August, students arranged themselves on the carpet as Elyse prepared for the 2nd-grade class's first journaling workshop. Anticipation of their new journal project had been building with phone calls and letters home. Elyse had explained each aspect of the process. They were ready to write home.

In the beginning, Elyse's class composed a letter together, Elyse wrote it on a chart, and students copied the letters in their journals. Some students struggled with copying and needed a printed version on their desk, so they could cross out words as they wrote. The following is an early entry:

> Dear, Family
>   This week we learne about predictions. We rean books and thought about what will happen what you predict I will be when grow up?

From the beginning, Elyse encouraged students to take ownership of their letters and personalize their work. Some began to add personal comments or make adaptations to the letter, like with the salutations and closings. One student addressed a letter, "Dear Red Apple," and his mom returned her response with, "Dear Love Muffin." Some students and parents included illustrations. One parent glued a map in her child's journal when responding to an entry that explained the state regions and asked, "Where did you grow up?" Several students created problems for their families to solve when journaling about a math topic, and many families returned the favor by creating related problems for their children to solve. Several students began including their own additional questions. When the class asked their families how they felt when they took a big test, one student also asked for suggestions to help her when she took tests.

As more students began adding their own touches to the letters, the class letter transitioned to a sample letter that did not have to be copied. Students referenced the class web of ideas to form their own letters, making sure to include the class-generated question. Eventually, students formed their own letters after generating the discussion, class question, and web of words and phrases. After learning about Dr. Martin Luther King in social studies and beginning their focus on persuasive reading and writing, Elyse's class asked, "How can I use the power of my words?" The web included facts about Dr. Martin Luther King as well as what it means to persuade. As a result, student letters began to take on individual form. One student wrote:

Dear mom,
    We were talking about MLK and persuasive peaces. A lot of people no that MLK had a lot of powerful words. Persuasive peaces are when charther [characters] try to perswad you to doing something for thing. One more thing how can we make MLK words powerful?

Another student wrote:

Derar Famley,
    How are you? I am good too. How can I use the power of my words? I can ofceve [achieve] my gole in the school becuz I'm good.

In April, Elyse's class reflected on how their process had changed through the year. At that time, her students expressed their desire to have more choice when it came to the question. They decided that they would now form two class questions, so students could choose to use one or both of the questions, such as, "How do you celebrate Earth Day?" or "What do you know about Earth Day?"

Classroom discussions and parent input helped guide the overall journaling process, but individual students' processes changed more frequently based on individual preferences, abilities, and needs. For example, when she changed grade levels, Elyse put different kinds of paper into each kindergartner's folder to support students' drawing and writing as they developed, allowing students who were ready to use more lines. As they became able, students took over more responsibilities, such as stapling the class-generated question into each journal.

Jennifer, like Elyse, came to realize that you have to create and revise your own process. "It feels like if I don't generate topics and questions like everyone else, or if I don't have the accountability or sharing routines they do, I'm doing it wrong. But there is no one right way to utilize FDJs in your classroom. You take what sounds like it will work for you, and try it out." Her students had also expressed some unhappiness with whole-class selected topics, but their transition to multiple topics came about differently.

Her class became the special education inclusion class midyear and gained another writing teacher, who later gained an intern. With three teachers in the classroom, there was room for students to generate three topic choices. Each teacher took a topic and a space in the room, then students wrote with the teacher leading their favorite topic. The students became more engaged, productive, and exhibited more enthusiasm. It was such fun that Jennifer's husband began volunteering in her classroom some Fridays to lead a fourth group!

At one point in her second year, Jennifer felt particularly stressed. She was involved in opening a new school and also teaching a new grade level. Her class was having difficulty in posing a question for the FDJs that might spark a meaningful conversation. JoBeth suggested that she create a classroom chart for students to write on during the week. Jennifer thought that would help her and her students in focusing on what they had learned and done throughout the week. Jennifer introduced the chart, "Things We Are Learning and Doing This Week," saying, "You know how on Fridays when we go to make a list of things we've learned for our journals? And sometimes we can't remember? Well, I thought if we made a chart each week, then anytime we learned something new or did something cool we could add it to the chart!" Students got excited. As they told her things they had learned, she sent them over to the chart to add it. After a few weeks, they didn't seem to need the chart. But trying out something new helped regenerate new passion for journals.

At the end of her first year implementing journals, Amber asked students and parents to evaluate the process. Both parents and students suggested that they do the journals every 2 weeks instead of every week. As Missy explained, "It takes time to plan and write a well-thought-out entry, and often, our parents do not have that much time every week." Amber realized that the journals may have been infringing on parents' busy schedules, and wanted the journals to be more enjoyable. Second, students expressed their preference for class-created prompts and said that they wanted more choice in their writing topics (a common theme!). Finally, students wanted the option to write to a larger audience; they wanted more choice in who could write in their journals.

Now confident that FDJs provided a meaningful link between parents, students, teachers, and the high school curriculum, Amber built on her previous year's experiences as well as student and parent suggestions to modify her use of FDJs for the next year.

- *More class-created prompts.* Because students said that they enjoyed "bouncing ideas off each other," Amber only provided one teacher-created prompt for students to use as a model and invited students to cocreate future topics. Because of this change, she found it necessary to teach and reinforce critical questioning during class discussion since she had less opportunity to do so when creating FDJ questions.
- *Responses due every 2 weeks instead of every week.* In addition to parent and student comments, a practical reason for changing the time frame was that Amber implemented FDJs with all of her AP classes during her second year, increasing her reading load from 14 journals to 65. Amber now had 2 weeks to respond, writing in about six journals a day. While this change in time frame resulted in fewer entries, Amber felt it resulted in happier students and parents and lengthier, more thoughtful responses.
- *More choice of writing topics.* Instead of requesting that students all write on the same topic, Amber encouraged students to choose

one of the three or four questions that students constructed during class, one they found most engaging or thought their family might want to write about. The questions generally addressed the same piece of literature or theme but differed in application to the world or students' experiences. Amber found the responses more personal due to the variety of questions and responses.

- *Option for wider audience.* Amber agreed to let individuals besides parents participate in responding in the FDJs, so long as they were outside of school. This alleviated her fear that students would not take the journals home. Students dialogued with aunts, uncles, brothers, sisters, grandparents, cousins, and so on, and members of their smaller communities such as their churches, synagogues, or mosques. With this change, participation increased significantly.

Even with these changes in how she implemented FDJs in her classroom during her second year, the FDJ process still supported Amber's goal to expand academic discussions among the teacher, students, and families. This encouraged her students to question dominant ideologies and oppressive language and actions in order to create more socially active and critically aware citizens.

First, more student-generated, class-created writing prompts did not decrease the critical nature of the questions. Below are some student-generated prompts from Amber's second year of implementing FDJs:

- We are currently studying satire and are about to read *The Importance of Being Earnest.* When is satire appropriate and when is it offensive?
- Do you think that people rely on religion so they don't have to question the unknown?
- Based on your own experiences, do you think there is a difference between how men and women communicate?

While giving a little less background knowledge as to the context of the question, students still focused on critical themes such as recognizing and avoiding offensive language, accepting human difference, and questioning the world and personal beliefs.

Second, giving students 2 weeks to respond seemed to make them more eager to engage in prompt creation and response sharing. Toward the end of the first year Amber implemented FDJs, students' responses became shorter in length, and class-created topics got "silly." In the second year, the length of responses remained consistent and the critical content of the questions became more serious. For example, the last question of the year was, "Is there such a thing as 'objective' reasoning that is untainted by cultural norms or assumptions of what is good and bad?" a question influenced by

President Obama's Cairo speech. This was, in Amber's opinion, the most challenging critical question of the year.

Third, even when writing on a variety of topics, students were still able to learn from one another's family experiences. For example, one class chose three questions when discussing critical issues in the *Harry Potter* series:

- Is it dangerous to put social issues in children's books?
- How do children's novels affect the status quo?
- How can we relate social class issues in Harry Potter to those we see today?

When the class discussed the questions, including family responses, one student shared her mother's point that parents and children should read together in order to discuss social issues in books. Another student discussed his parent's' experience teaching middle school and seeing students "grouped" according to economic class.

Finally, to Amber's surprise and delight, allowing students to include more participants actually encouraged them to engage in critical dialogue in multiple communities. For example, when discussing *Heart of Darkness* students wrote about a time when they realized the "horror" of their actions. One Ethiopian student, Amina, shared her sister's story about going against her culture's norms and getting married at the court instead of having a big family wedding. She talked about her mother's disappointment, and how she regretted it because she did not know how much it would hurt her mother. We were able to include her perspective (the cultural "delinquent") as well as Amina's perspective when the class discussed parents' expectations for children to follow cultural norms. Another time, when questioning whether the West valued Eastern cultures, Mahti solicited the opinion of a member of her mosque. They concluded that the West was not truly "globalized," and called for more education on world religions and cultures. Mahti revealed, "I think that living in America, I have a bias on the definition of globalization. I think of the East adopting Western practices." This realization that she, a follower of a traditionally Eastern religion, was complicit in the West's domination over Eastern culture, is high-level critical thinking. Because Mahti was able to discuss this topic with someone outside her family—a friend from her own age group, culture, and religion—she was able to question candidly her own beliefs about her unbalanced relationship with Eastern and Western thought.

Amber's experience reinforces the claim that there is no one way to implement Family Dialogue Journals. In fact, being willing to change and negotiate enhances the experience of everyone involved. In the next chapter, you'll see how parents both responded to journal entries and shaped the evolution of the FDJ process.

Mini-Lesson Idea: Questioning

Prior to Lesson

- Write questions previously used in the journaling process or teacher-generated questions that elicit open and closed responses on sentence strips.
- Create a T-chart labeled Types of Questions, with Open Question and Closed Question headings.

Opening

1. Students will share with two different partners. For each round of sharing, students are given 1 minute to find a partner and share their responses. Round One: partners share when/where they are often asked questions and why they think that is. Round Two: partners share when/where they often ask questions and why they think that is.
2. Bring students together and share some of the responses from each round.

Mini-Lesson

1. Explain that we will be considering the types of questions we ask with regard to the responses elicited by each question. Complicate the examples and the range of question types for older students.
2. Show an example, such as, "Can you add 13 + 13?" Ask students how someone might respond to the question. Place the question under the "closed question" half of the t-chart because it can be answered yes or no or with the sum.
3. Show an example, such as, "When do you use addition in your life?" Ask students how someone might respond to the question. Place the question under the "open question" half of the t-chart because it can be answered in several ways, depending on personal experiences.
4. Have students work in pairs for 2 to 3 minutes to determine how to sort three questions, placing their questions on the class t-chart.
5. Review the chart and open a class dialogue regarding what types of questions we should be asking when we write home and why. Why might an open question be used? Why might a closed question be used?
6. Explain that we will be writing home today regarding questioning. Have students help you form a question. Model thinking aloud to check whether the question is open or closed. Encourage students to form their own open question about questioning.

Student Work

Students write letters home in their journals, making sure to include the class generated or self-generated question.

Closing

Review the purpose of an open question and a closed question as discussed earlier in the lesson. Ask students a series of questions to check their abilities to distinguish the two types of questions using hand motions—hands apart to mean open and hands together to signify closed. For example:

1. What state do we live in?
2. What was school like when you were in the 3rd grade?

CHAPTER 4

Going Home

Families Read, Discuss, and Respond

Fridays are a special day in Family Dialogue Journal classrooms. That's the day the journals go home. That's the invitation to families to talk with their children about some particular and important concept, issue, or theme they've been studying the previous week or two. That's the day students get to ask family members, "What is your experience? Your perspective? Your advice?"

FAMILY RESPONSE PROCESSES

Many of Elyse's kindergarten families commented on how they enjoyed reading the entries together because their children often provided additional information and stories related to the entries. Other families said reading the journals together provided an enjoyable way of practicing both reading and writing with their children. The younger children were able to read more and more of the entries independently as the year progressed. One mother expressed her pride in how much her daughter learned, as demonstrated in the journal each week. Then, the mother expressed concern for her older child, who was experiencing much frustration in school. The parent and teacher talked about possibilities, including having her son respond to his little sister's journal entries. Although he did not write regularly, he responded from time to time. One journal allowed two siblings to practice reading and writing in an authentic manner.

Students chose to write to a variety of family members in and out of their primary residence: moms, dads, grandparents, siblings, uncles, and aunts. This choice impacted how a family responded. There were times when students addressed their letters to their dad, and their mom would respond instead. Other times, a student wrote, "To Mom and Dad" and both parents would respond. One kindergartner in Elyse's class decided to write to her 4-year-old cousin. Teresa's grandmother read the letter to her younger cousin who dictated her response to Grandma, who wrote it in Teresa's journal. Students were learning that they had choices as writers—choice of topics, purposes, and audiences.

In the beginning of each year, most of Jennifer's students addressed letters to their mom or dad. A few wrote to an older brother or sister because their parents didn't have time to respond or couldn't write in English. Jennifer explained to her students that any family member could write in Spanish, which a bilingual staff member could translate. A few parents started writing in Spanish; others had their child write for them in English.

Elizabeth, a 2nd-grader, included her extended family in this and subsequent letters.

Dear Family,
　　　Today is Earth Day! We sang about Earth Day. We watched a video about earth Day. Earth Day reminds us to recycle, reuse, reduse, care for natural resources and take care of the Planet. How do you care for the Planet at home. Love,

Elizabeth

Elizabeth's mom wrote: (translated from Spanish)

At home the way I help the planet is by recycling the bottles and bags in a special container and that way I help the environment. If we all cooperated the planet would not be contaminated.

Elizabeth's aunt wrote (translated from Spanish):

In my house we recycle all the bottles and aluminum cans and any metals that we don't use and take it to the recycling center. We clean and pick up everything that we don't use and that's how we help to keep our planet clean.

Elizabeth's uncle wrote (translated from Spanish):

We can all help with keeping our planet healthy—one way is to recycle trash and separate items better lightbulbs and I only recharge my phone for two hours.

The Importance of Home Language

Two-thirds of Jen's students spoke Spanish at home, and the rest spoke English. She was lucky to have a coteacher, Mr. Oswaldo, whose native language was Spanish, and he translated her students' focal question(s) from English to Spanish each week, as well as parents' Spanish responses into English. This meant all of the children's families could read and respond to the students' inquiries in the language with which they were most comfortable. Attention to the linguistic diversity present in her classroom was important to Jen, as she wanted to ensure that all students and their families could participate in Family Dialogue Journals. This led to an interesting development in family responses, one she had not anticipated.

Hector and his mother, Elena, regularly discussed each journal's weekly topic or question. Their family's language was Spanish, which meant that while Hector wrote the bulk of his response in English, Mr. Oswaldo translated his question into Spanish. After Hector and Jen read a few of Elena's responses aloud during Morning Meeting, Jen began to notice that Elena addressed the entire class in her greeting. "*Buenos días para todos*/Good morning to all," she would write, before penning detailed paragraphs in response to the class's question. Elena saw her audience as all of the students; most other mothers, fathers, siblings, or other community members addressed only their child.

Jen asked Elena about this during fall family conferences, as they talked about whether she was continuing to enjoy the Family Dialogue Journal process, since this was their second year engaging in this communication. Elena assured Jen that she loved sharing her background and beliefs with the class, and she treasured the time she spent contemplating and writing her responses to the children's questions.

"Do you and Hector talk about what he wrote?" Jen asked.

Laughing, Elena responded with the help of a translator, "No, he just drops the journal and runs outside to play!"

They laughed together, envisioning the blur that was Elena's son, dark curls bouncing and uniform jumbled after a full day at school, jumping off the bus and tossing the journal on their counter. Although Jen and the students had discussed the importance of talking with families about what they wrote each week, Jen knew that not all students would do this.

It dawned on Jen that Elena, who was literate in Spanish, could only read the *question* in Hector's journal entries. He wrote his own words in English, and although he addressed each letter to Elena, this made them largely inaccessible to her. Since the two did not discuss what Hector wrote, Elena based her responses on the single-sentence inquiries. This question was rather impersonal, written so that it reflected the entire class's wonderings, and accounted for Elena's tendency to formally respond to the entire class, rather than only to her son.

With this in mind, Jen encouraged Hector to talk with his family about what he wrote each week, telling him that this could be a way for his mother to learn how to write in English and for him to learn to read and write in Spanish. Jen also reminded Hector, Naldo, and Christopher, who had previously shown an interest in bilingual entries, that they could sit together as they wrote their journals to support and assist one another in Spanish writing.

With his middle school students who were struggling with school in multiple ways, Joseph encouraged native Spanish speakers to write in Spanish. He also challenged himself to dialogue with these students and their families in Spanish. He was not a fluent Spanish speaker, but doggedly wrote each in Spanish, encouraging his students to help him express his ideas. Because several of his students were recent immigrants, Joseph encouraged them to develop biliteracy. They seemed to appreciate Joseph's efforts at learning their native language as they were learning his. Joseph felt he not only improved his rudimentary Spanish but also formed a more trusting and reciprocal relationship with students and families by communicating in Spanish.

Students and Families Take Different Approaches

Through the mistaken greeting to a classmate ("Dear Malik") rather than a family member in Jennifer's classroom, one journal did not make it home. It sparked a new phenomenon! As she tried to think of a way to delicately tell the student that family journals need to be addressed to family, not classmates, she thought, "Why not? If he wants to write to his friend, couldn't I just give them a journal to share?" As the boys were choosing the color for their new journal out of her supply closet, other students gathered around. Two girls asked, "Can we share a friend journal?" "Sure!" Jennifer replied. Students bunched up to form pairs all over the room and started making their way to the supply closet. As journals were grabbed and students tried to decide who would write first, Jennifer told the students that this would be their own project, done on their own time. They had complete ownership. They were exhilarated and so was Jennifer. Can you imagine how students would have reacted if she had *assigned* extracurricular writing?

At the high school level, students described varying processes regarding how their family participated in the journal. Some of Amber's students said that they wrote their entry and left the journal on a specific table or counter for the parent to respond in at their convenience. Other students, like Beth, discussed the prompt with her family at dinner before writing her own thoughts down and inviting her parents to write. This gave the family time to informally talk and brainstorm their response before constructing a written reply. In other families, like Elliot's, his mother took his journal with her on business trips and responded during her flight. Likewise, Kali's dad sometimes took the journal to work with him and responded during his free time. Based on her discussion with students on their family's response process, Amber came to the conclusion that, once again, there is no one "right" FDJ writing process. Each process is unique depending on the dynamics and schedules of individual families.

Most of the time, parents of Angela's students wrote directly in the journals, but sometimes Angela opened the journal to find parents writing in their home language and the student's translation below. There were also times when the student might interview the parent and write for them because of time constraints. Several students chose to write to siblings rather than their parents. One student really wanted to dialogue with her cousin, but he lived in California so Angela and Viridiana decided that Viridiana could use email and phone calls to complete the journal.

In the FDJ survey Angela sent home, she asked students how the process went for them and what they might change. Jorge responded: "The process went very well for me. I liked how you took the time and read every single entry and responded back to it. I feel it would have been better if it was just a two-way connection rather than a three way."

Angela made allowances for such instances so that participation in the journals stayed as consistent as possible. There were also a few students who had slow starts and students who started strong and missed a few entries during the semester. Angela always allowed for students to go back to topics they may have missed and write about them. For her, the process and participation were very important, so to find ways of meeting her students' and families' needs during the project was most important.

Figuring Out How to Respond

Angela found that her own responses were at times easy to provide and at others, very difficult. In looking across the journals, there were entries where Angela clearly made a connection with what the child and family have shared. For instance, Sierra focused on a weekly tradition in her home as well as a yearly tradition like the examples from Garrett and Camilla in Chapter 2. "One of the traditions we have is every Sunday the meal that is prepared is rice and peas, stew chicken, and potato salad." Sierra's mother expanded on the weekly tradition of the Sunday meal:

> For decedents of West Indian culture, the Sunday meal is very important. The meal will consist of several different dishes, but what is expected to be included are potato salad, stewed chicken and rice and peas. Each generation is given the opportunity to learn how to prepare these dishes to perpetuate this tradition for years to come.

Angela found it quite easy to draw upon her own upbringing:

> Sunday dinner is a tradition my family had when I was growing up too. We'd come home from church and my mom would make a big lunch—warm lunch, with meat and veggies. In the summer, the vegetables were typically taken from the garden. The meat was usually venison or maybe a roast. You'd be so full, you had to go take a nap. Sometimes we might stop by a restaurant on the way home that served traditional Southern foods like fried chicken or country fried steak, biscuits, and banana pudding, but typically we would eat at home around our dining room table. When we did go out, the banana pudding was my favorite!

Though this particular entry is not a challenging or invasive question, there were times when Angela found herself opening up to a family in ways she had not expected. One such instance was in an exchange with Julian and his mother.

The question focused on losing hope and it came toward the end of the semester, when the class was reading *They Poured Fire on Us from the Sky* (Deng, Deng, Ajak, & Bernstein 2005). In the book, three "lost boys" survive the genocide in the country now known as South Sudan. Their harrowing narratives pushed the students to consider challenges they had faced in their own lives. The question about losing hope came at a time when the three boys were separated and had no way of knowing if they would ever see each other or their other family members again; at times they doubted if they would make it to the next day. This question was developed from reading and discussion around the book and the boys' experiences with losing hope. Julian considered the question, "At what times have you lost hope? Why?" His response:

> There [were] many times I lost hope last year. I lost hope in football because I didn't try. But now I'm off to a good start and I'm going to keep it up. I lost hope in growing since my dad is short and my mom is short and I've been the same height since 8th grade. Other kids were always taller and bigger but I've grown to know I don't have control over my height. People used to tell me to hang from a bar so all my limbs could stretch out . . . It didn't work. People told me if I slept a lot, then you will grown because people grow in their sleep. I slept every day to stay the same since I am now. ☹

Julian, like many adolescent boys, had hopes of going to college to play football and perhaps make it to the National Football League. While struggling with height is not equivalent to never seeing one's family again, Julian was still sharing his struggle to come to terms with something he had no control over. Julian's mother responded:

> I lost hope in Corp. America in the dream of having a job that would last until I retired, after I was promoted to manager after 4 years with [Company], they laid my whole department off.

Having lived in a home where family members also faced setbacks with work, Angela felt that she understood what Julian's mom might have felt:

> Set backs like losing jobs can be really difficult. Mr. Dean has been forced to transfer in the county two years in a row. This year has been tough because it seemed that no one had a job opening at their school.

All we heard was that schools were losing people—not hiring. The not knowing took its toll on us and it has been a difficult two years. We've had to reevaluate what we value and what we believe. We've also had to be hopeful. It isn't easy when there seems to be nothing out there. I try to stay positive, but it is hard. My stepfather lost his job when I was 8 or 9 years old. It was a really stressful time and I can understand the frustration of feeling the dream is lost. Starting over was tough for him and it has been tough for Mr. Dean. I hope that things will get better for us in America soon.

Sharing personal feelings and stories is a vulnerable act. In this exchange, Angela felt that Julian's mother, even with only two lines, had opened up about what she was facing at home. Angela responded with similarly personal details.

In the secondary classroom, the topics of discussion are often challenging and at times, deeply personal. Negotiating the dialogic space in the family journals can be difficult. Being open, however, was not as easy for other students or even for Angela all of the time. In one exchange with Jimmy, Angela found herself holding back.

The central narrator of *Bronx Masquerade* (Grimes, 2002), Tyrone, has little time for school and sees no value in education. Angela and the students looked critically at why Tyrone held this view of school and how his views challenged or related to their own experiences. Students coconstructed several writing options, but many chose the prompt about education. Many felt that their parents were going to give their standard speeches on school and education; they wanted to word the question so that their parents would answer truthfully. Jimmy's question was, "Do you believe education is important to everyone? What classes or teachers influenced you?" Jimmy answered:

I believe education is only as important as the individual makes it. I don't believe that race, economic class, etc. have that much of an affect on whether someone values education. Ultimately, it depends on the way the individual thinks.

Jimmy's mother wrote:

I do believe education is important for everyone. Everyone needs to learn at least the basic skills of reading and math to be independent, functioning, and productive citizens as adults regardless of their goals for adult life. I wish our current educational system provided more choices for students today because not everyone is headed to college. In addition, for our country to remain competitive and ranked highest amongst other countries, all of our people need to be educated.

Angela wanted to pick up on Jimmy's mother's critique of the school system and really be candid, but was unsure about expressing a very critical view. She tried to find a balance between being cautious and expressing her feelings.

> I would agree with the frustration in having a single-track/one-size-fits-all curriculum. I wish that more had been done with developing the technical track instead of doing away with it. I'd also like to see more opportunities for kids to try courses or internships in high school so that they could test their knowledge in areas they really value. Again and again I hear students complain that they don't see a connection to the courses they take and the things they want to do.

Angela could have detailed her frustrations, but was concerned about taking a stance that was too critical of the system. As she read through the responses about education, she wanted to say more herself and wanted to encourage parents and students to speak up about their frustrations. She remained torn about how critical she could be of her employers in the journal, and she held back on some of her opinions.

CREATING DIALOGIC THREADS

In *most* classrooms, *most* families responded *most* of the time—that's a lot of mosts! Many of the journal entries elicited great conversation for the next 5 days during their sharing, but then rarely continued past that week. We teachers might refer back to a journal topic or parent response in casual conversation and students did the same, but every week there seemed to be another interesting topic that would steal our attention. However, some topics generated longer discussion, creating dialogic threads that wove in and out of the journals, homes, and our classrooms.

Learning New Math

One extended conversation happened in Stephanie's 4th-grade class when the students wrote home to parents teaching them how to solve division problems in their new way. For several weeks, students included a problem and asked parents to show them how they solved the problem their way. Students then showed them the new way they learned in class that they referred to as the "4th grade way." KenAsia wrote, "Dear mom, We are learning about division . . . When you are doing division you can use the 4th grade strategy." At the conclusion of her letter she asked her mom, "Can you show me how you would solve 59 ÷ 4?" KenAsia then showed her mother the steps for division:

First we write a hangman and put the numbers inside. Then we draw our groups to the side. Not too big, not too small, but just right. Next we ask ourselves 'Can we take groups of 10?' 5? 2? When you can't take out any more equal groups, the rest is a remainder."

KenAsia correctly solved the math problem and then drew a line down the middle of her paper so her mom's way could be on the other side. Her mom solved the problem on her side of the paper using the traditional algorithm.

Because the two algorithms are so different, the students were shocked at how their parents learned to divide and the parents were equally shocked at this new way. One parent, bound and determined to learn their new way to solve division problems, showed up to their math class one day and stayed for over an hour learning their class's strategy for division. She later told Stephanie, "I knew if I was going to help my daughter in math, I was going to need to learn how she was doing math."

This journal dialogue also had a profound effect upon Dan'ia as a learner. Dan'ia came into the class as a struggling math student, saying repeatedly, "I'm no good in math." Because Dan'ia's mom took such an interest in her learning, Dan'ia put forth a huge effort to learn to divide and met all of the division standards. Dan'ia, her mother, and Stephanie were all so proud.

A Sustained Dialogue About Gender

A family dialogue journal is a continuous conversation, and the goal is to create a dialogic thread that can be revisited at the participants' discretion. When responding to FDJ entries, Amber created a dialogic thread by asking questions of the students and parents, encouraging them to elaborate on a particular observation or nudging them to reconsider a position by looking at it from another perspective. Below is an example of such a dialogic thread from Beth's journal in response to a prompt about gender bias:

> *Beth:* In Faulkner's novel *As I Lay Dying* the social class issues were that women had to be submissive to their husbands. The men worked outside of the house and brought in the money for the family while the women stayed at home and cooked and took care of the house and children. The submission to the husband is discussed in Cora's chapter when she messed up and must tell Tull what she has done. The idea of a patriarchal society rarely exists in today's society. In today's society men and women have equal rights and equal opportunities such as voting and equal pay for equal work. Women in today's society are not just confined to the household to cook, clean, and take care of the children. They are given the opportunity to go to college to get an

education to earn a job to earn money for their family. Do you feel that this change in society is for the better or worse? Why or why not?

Beth's father: This change is for the better. Everybody should have the freedom and right to a higher education and become a productive member of society.

Beth's mother: I feel this change is for the better. I think that it is good for both men and women to be able to both work and provide for the family. I grew up where my mom didn't work and my dad did. He died suddenly and she had difficulty going into the workforce.

Amber: You bring up a good point that poverty is linked to gender. The poorest people in the U.S. are single mothers, or at least they are one of the highest populations of people below the poverty line. How does that fact challenge your statement about opportunities for women in today's society?

Beth: Single mothers don't have two incomes for their families and they can't go back to school to get a better degree to get a better job because they are raising their children alone. Those women have the same opportunities yet they have an obligation to raising their children.

Amber: So how does a woman balance obligation and opportunity? In a way, are they still confined?

Referring to the mother's comment about single mothers, Amber asked Beth to assess her statement about equal opportunity through a more critical lens. When the journals came back the next week, Beth, very dialogically, gave credence to Amber's question, yet still seemed to be in agreement with her father that higher education was the way to become a productive member of society. When Amber asked her final question, which used Beth's own description of women being "confined," Amber tried to draw the parallel between the confinement of mothers "back then" and today's single mothers. However, perhaps uninterested or unwilling to shatter the ideology that things are "all better" now, Beth did not accept the invitation to continue the dialogue in the journal. However, while the thread ended in the journal, the issue was brought up during class discussion where other students gave their opinion on the opportunities available to single mothers, which opened up the dialogue that began with Beth's family to the larger classroom community.

Amber also realized that sustained threads of dialogue could occur in a more subtle manner. Alim, who was relating the events in Egypt to those in

The Da Vinci Code, wrote, "Brown presents examples of restricting women to subordinate roles by powerful Catholic men, just as the Egyptians were oppressed by their powerful leader," revealing how women in the Catholic church were suppressed since they could not hold any high positions in the orders. After Alim, his parents, and Amber responded to this prompt, it was never revisited in his journal. However, the dialogue occurred thematically because the prompt from a previous week questioned the role of women in society. This response shows how the student continued the conversation about gender bias and his desire to discuss this social inequality as he recognized its existence in other works of literature, inviting his parents and Amber to maintain the dialogue.

Dialogic Threads from Class to Journal to Home Discussion

During a discussion about ideology and how we adopt beliefs based on what is considered the cultural norm and "tradition," Amber and her students broached the topic of whether or not people should stand for the Pledge of Allegiance, whether they believed in the words or not. This launched a dialogue on the exact words of the pledge, including "one nation under God" and "liberty and justice for all." One student, Evelyn, stated that she did not believe that those words were truthful. "There is not liberty and justice for all and until there is, I won't stand up." Other students said that the pledge was a national tradition and you should stand even if you did not believe in the words. One student said that if she were in a culture that required her to take off her shoes before entering a house or cover her head in public, she would do it in order to show respect for their culture. She said that she expected the same when it came to the pledge. She said standing to show respect for our tradition does not mean they have to actually say the words if they don't believe them. One student asked if he could choose this topic as a journal prompt. Knowing that many students did not have an opportunity to express their thoughts and share their experiences on this issue, Amber agreed. About a third of the class wrote on this prompt. Christy's response stood out:

> I especially loved this day in Lang class last week. In all my other classes we usually don't talk about subject matters that cause controversy, and so any day that we have Socratic seminar is especially interesting. When we have these discussions, it seems that my opinions are sometimes somewhat different than my other classmates when discussing the pledge of allegiance. I think that the pledge of allegiance is an American tradition that shows our country's unification. Our country seems to forget that we have soldiers fighting for us across the ocean. Emphasis on their effort is no longer breaking news in America and it is sad that they are not given as much credit as they deserve.

Although the pledge seems outdated to some, I'm sure these men and women overseas appreciate the short thirty seconds given to represent them and their country each morning. The recital of the pledge takes no time out of anyone's day and if it is the only recognition that our soldiers get in twenty four hours, then they deserve it. However, I understand where some of the class is coming from when they say it means nothing and no one understands what is actually coming out of their mouth. I think that this is due to the lack of emphasis people place on it when we first learn it. We are only taught to memorize and recite, not digest the meaning of the words.

Christy's mother: As a former kindergarten teacher/first-grade teacher, I absolutely believe that our classroom day should begin with reciting the pledge of allegiance. It is one of the few ways that Americans can unite together and show our pride and respect for our country. It helps us honor those who gave their lives so that we all have our freedoms. It also helps us show support for those that continue to fight our enemies so that our freedom continues. As a teacher, I know my young students don't understand all I have stated. So I would try to make it easier for them. We talked about how they honor and respect their parents and teachers. We talk about going to church and honoring God. We say the pledge to honor our country and its history. Then we would talk about the words in the pledge and what they mean on a very simple scale. Then I would set the example by standing straight and tall.

Amber's response: I am glad to see that the discussion resonated with you and that you considered your peers' point of view. I agree that the pledge means a lot to our troops and to many other Americans. However, if our troops are fighting for our freedoms, do you think they would agree with people not having the freedom to sit and not say the pledge? I think that, like your mom said, teaching respect is very important, but I also think that we should not only memorize, recite, and digest the meaning of the words, but also question them. If they can't stand up to questioning, are they really as significant as we think?

Christy's response resonated with Amber because it showed that while the student ultimately sided with the dominant cultural belief, she was willing to try to understand others' points of view. She did not discredit their beliefs by saying "they're wrong" or "that's stupid," common teenage responses during debate. Instead she tried to position herself in her peers' frame of mind and consider why they might feel the way they do, even though she did not share that feeling. Christy expressed a critical shift in her dialogic skills through her FDJ. Amber's response pushed her to take her critical development to the next step through further questioning. Christy's response showed another important aspect of dialogic threads: dialogue on this potentially divisive topic began in the classroom, moved to the journals, and continued at home, allowing family members to share their perspectives, and then wove back into the classroom conversation as students shared responses from their parents.

WHY DIDN'T SOMEONE AT HOME RESPOND?

It happens. It happened to all of us at times—a student forgot to take the journal home (or out of her backpack), parents were too busy to respond, we as teachers lost a week or two here and there to time pressures. But there were several situations when we weren't getting responses from home that taught us to dig deeper into why.

Each week, Elyse's 2nd-grade classroom became more streamlined and consistent with the procedural elements of the journaling process—journals went home on Friday and returned the following week, most by Wednesday. However, students returned a few journals without a response. Early in the week, Elyse's simple reminder to students to share their journal with any member of their family was often enough. This reminder included practicing how to bring the journal to a family member and possibilities of what to say. "Dad, we rewrote fairy tales at school. I wrote to you about it in my journal. I want to know how you would rewrite the same story." Or "Grandma, I wrote you a letter in my journal. Can you write back to me? Here it is." Sometimes this reminder also included practicing how not to give their journals to their families, such as tossing the journal on a table and running outside to play. However, practice and reminders were not always enough.

One student, Sharron, did not bring her journal back with comments for 2 weeks in a row. Elyse asked Sharron what they could do, and Sharron said that she just wanted to write to different people. Elyse called Sharron's mom after school to ask how she felt about Sharron writing to previous teachers and siblings in addition to writing with her. Her mom was okay with the idea as long as Sharron participated and completed her work. That Friday, Sharron immediately began writing in her journal, addressing her letter to a 1st-grade teacher. She excitedly walked the journal to the teacher on her way to recess. Monday morning, the journal was waiting in Elyse's mailbox in the office, so she placed it on Sharron's desk. Sharron beamed with joy when she read the response. Each week Sharron chose her audience, usually teachers or staff at school, a sibling, or her mom. For Sharron, all she wanted was the choice of audience.

Mark, another student, required more problem-solving for his journaling drought. Elyse and Mark practiced how to give the journal to a family member, but Mark continued to say that his mother would not write back to him. The teacher suggested that Mark try writing to teachers, siblings, and even to her husband. Mark expressed a clear desire to write to his mother and reiterated that his mother would not write back. Mark's mother had always been responsive when the teacher called or wrote home, so Elyse met with her about the journals. His mother appeared shocked that her son would think that she would not write back. "He told me I was only supposed to sign my name!" They talked about the journaling process and purpose with Mark's journal in front of them, then Elyse gave her the journal. The following week, Mark placed his journal on Elyse's table. His smile stretched ear to ear as he asked if he could share during Morning Meeting. That morning, and almost every week following, Mark shared from his journal.

As we discussed dilemmas such as Mark's in our study group, Jennifer realized that she had no idea who had consistent dialogue with their mom, who asked their reluctant sister weekly to please write something, or who just kept the journal hidden in their backpack. Students put their journals in a basket each morning, which she took to Morning Meeting. After sharing, students put their journals on her desk for a response. But she had neglected to keep any record of who shared or brought in their journal weekly. She quickly devised an easy checklist system so she could monitor participation, follow up as needed with students or parents, and prevent a student from feeling detached or ignored.

Having each other to bounce ideas off, both in our monthly meetings and on our FDJ wiki, helped us address (if not always solve) issues such as ones Stephanie encountered from a few families.

"Ms. Smith, I found my son's weekend journal at the bottom of his laundry basket. Is he still supposed to be writing in it?"

"We never did these at my old school. Do we *have* to do them?"

"I like the family weekend journals but my mom don't have time to sign it and when she do have time to sign she forget to sign it."

We would be remiss if honest comments such as these were left out of our discussion of family journals. Quite frankly, we're don't know the answers for making this successful for all students and their families. We will, however, address a few possible reasons for the lack of responses.

We must first look at our definition of success. We wanted to construct written dialogue between student, family, and teacher that created opportunities for learning and understanding. However, Stephanie had a few students who rarely brought back a response from their family in the journal, although the students wrote weekly in their journal. When asked to reflect upon the experience with the journal, Brandon responded, "I like writing in my family weekend journal." Perhaps for him this was a safe place to write. Perhaps his idea of success was writing in his journal each week.

There are a multitude of possibilities regarding why students don't give their parents the journal or why parents don't write in them. Outside pressure such as work, especially when parents are working multiple jobs or long, unconventional hours could make the task of writing in family journals with their child challenging. Perhaps when faced with a myriad of other priorities, family weekend journals just didn't make it onto the list. Some students may feel apprehensive about sharing their journals with their parents, and some parents, while enjoying hearing what their child wrote each week, might feel apprehensive about writing a response in the journal. Writing is, after all, still seen by many as something to be judged. We hope that like us, you seek to understand each challenge and work at finding a solution that supports your students and their families.

That is what Amber did. While she knew that parents were reading their students' entries, she was unsure if parents actually read her response to the previous week's entry before addressing the current week's prompt. In many cases, she asked parents direct questions about their response or their child, and she did not receive an answer. However, she knew that students read her responses religiously because of their sustained dialogic threads. Amber realized that she had done herself a disservice by not stating in her parent letter that she would be responding to their writing. She realized that the parents might think that what she wrote in the journal is meant for the student, not them, so they did not read it. Amber realized that she could have better prepared parents for sustained dialogue if she had encouraged questioning between students, teachers, and parents.

There were times for all of us when parents did not respond or didn't open up to the topic or question. Amber also noted times when students did not want to share with parents because the topic and the students' responses might have challenged relationships. While reading *They Poured Fire on Us from the Sky* (Deng et al., 2005), Amber's students noticed how close the three boys were to certain members of their families. Specifically, they were touched by the ways Benson Deng wrote about his mother and father. Camilla focused an entry on parent-child relationships, but chose not to share her entry with her mother. She wrote:

> This topic to me is very serious and deep. So I might not tell you a lot, but enough to tell you how I feel. My parents and I love each other, of course, but at times I feel like I'm not good enough for them. We have a great relationship, and all but there are those breaking points. When those problems start to occur the guilt all comes down on me. I feel like everything is my fault, and that I'm a disappointment to my family. I know those aren't their intentions to make me feel like that, but I get that feeling myself. It sucks because I want to be the best—I just hate the way I am at times. Like with an attitude, and the "I

don't give a crap" attitude, because I know that is not me, but I can't
help the way that side of me just comes out. I want to be perfect for
everyone, but it doesn't seem to want to happen. Yes, it bums me out,
and that's why I've been bummed out in class recently but I just want
to make them happy. And it's hard to change the way I am, because
that's me and changing the person you're used to, seems to be very
difficult . . . .what is the relationship you and your parents share?"

Camilla asked her friend Valerie to answer her journal. Valerie responded, "My parents and I share a very close relationship. I tell them everything
and share the most important things to them. Just how the kids in the book
share meals and learn new things from their parents, my parents do the
same with me and I enjoy that."
    Angela respected Camilla's wish not to share this entry with her mother,
even though in reading other entries Angela felt that Camilla's mom would
most likely understand and want to hear about Camilla's struggles so that
she could support her. Hoping to encourage Camilla, Angela wrote:

It is tough to negotiate relationships. My mom and I were close when I
was young. There are times now that I feel like we are really far apart
even when we are sitting next to each other. It is tough not to hurt
those close to you and lash out at them, but I know how touched your
mom was the other night when she saw all of your hard work. Both
your mom and Valerie's mom sat with huge smiles as they watched
your culture projects. Definitely not a disappointment. Keep your chin
up and keep working at the relationship you want to have with them.

For another student, it took a special prompt for him to share the journal at home. Jorge and Angela wrote back and forth for most of the year,
but Jorge did not take the journal home to share with a family member until
mid-March. The prompt required that students interview a family member about their name and why it was chosen for them. It also required the
students to write about how they felt about their names, the people they
may have been named after, and whether they might wish they were named
something else. This entry coincided with the reading of a chapter from
Bronx Masquerade (Grimes, 2002), where a student feels her name does not
identify who she feels she is on the inside. Angela coupled this chapter with
Sandra Cisneros' chapter from *The House on Mango Street* (1991) entitled
"My Name." In response to the prompt, Jorge wrote:

My name tells people that I am Hispanic. There's a reasons I prefer
people calling me "George" [quotations added] because people either
mispronounce my name or make fun of me because of the way my
name sounds. In my house my parents call me Isaac, my middle name.

It was supposed to be my real name but my grandmother wanted it to be Jorge so that I would be named after my great-uncle. If I could change my name I wouldn't, but I guess it's only because I don't know what I would change it to.

Angela is not certain why Jorge decided to have his mother write for this particular prompt. He was able to answer the questions himself. Perhaps it was the importance of the person he was named after and his wanting his mother to be able to tell her story of his uncle. Regardless, he finally took the journal home. Jorge's mother wrote:

I named my son Jorge after my uncle. I even think it was meant to be because my son born the same day of my uncle's birthday, December 18.
   My uncle was like a father to me, my sister, and brothers, him and my mother had a very nice relationship. He passed away when I was twelve years old; all the family was very sad after the loss. My uncle will always have a special place in my heart and thoughts.

Angela responded:

Your uncle sounds like he continues to be significant even though he's no longer alive and I am sure that Jorge carries on his name in a way that honors who he was. Jorge, what stories have you heard about him? What are some similarities you have in common with him?
   I too carry a special name. My parents named me Angela Marie. Marie represents my mother's first name, Mary. I'm very honored to have her name, but I didn't know that I was named for her until just a few years ago. I never really put it all together because my mother doesn't go by her first name; she goes by her middle name, Caroline. I knew her first name, but because no one calls her that I guess I just never considered that my middle name is a version of Mary. I am honored to be named after my mother and as I get to be older, I see how much I have of her inside of me. I am ashamed to say that I haven't always loved the name Marie, but now that I understand the significance of that name, I cherish it.

We share these examples, not because you will encounter the same ones, but because we suspect you will encounter different ones. The point is that we viewed each lack of response as an opportunity to better understand a student and/or family, to adapt the process for an individual or the whole class. We didn't say—and we know you won't say—"Journals may work with some students, but not mine." We constantly inquired into the process and modified it to make FDJs more beneficial for students, families, and our learning both in and out of school. Joseph continued even when only a handful of students seemed to benefit.

THE STARFISH

Let's be honest: Family Dialogue Journals are not embraced by all students, as Joseph taught our group. Most of Joseph's middle schools students, whom he saw irregularly as their graduation coach, showed little engagement with the journals. While Joseph was disappointed and frustrated, he concluded that offering the journals was worth the effort for those students who did engage.

Savannah was one such student. Her guardian, whom she referred to as Mom, was active in the school as a member of the PTO and frequent visitor. However, the journal opened up a new avenue of communication, one that focused directly on her child's school success. This mother shared her appreciation for the communication and the topics, stating that while she and her husband made every attempt to convey the importance of school, good grades, and appropriate behavior, many of the conversations in the dialogue journals were ones they would not have had otherwise. For example, the students watched a video about a group of high school students from another state who had dropped out of school. They talked about how boring school had been and frustrations with teachers, administrators, rules, and homework; they then made comparison to the boredom of sitting at home with nothing to do, inability to find work, fear, anxieties, and lack of information on how to go back to school.

As a result of the video and group conversation, the students decided to ask in the journal, "What was school like for you and did you ever think about dropping out?" In the journal, Savannah's mom shared her difficulties as a teenager and frustrations in school, and explained why she was so adamant about seeing her children succeed. Later that same week, the mother visited Joseph. She shared that she, her husband, and Savannah had never talked about their lives growing up and what their families' had been through. The three of them exchanged a few tears and hugs. Mom told Joseph that she didn't expect "drastic improvements in some of Savannah's tempers," but she now had greater faith that "Savannah will blossom into a productive young lady that we do not have to worry about."

Savannah was Joseph's "starfish." Readers, perhaps you remember the story (Eiseley, 1979) that has been retold in many different versions to illustrate why people persevere when a task seems daunting.

An old man had a habit of early morning walks on the beach. One day, after a storm, he saw a human figure in the distance moving like a dancer. As he came closer he saw that it was a young woman and she was not dancing but was reaching down to the sand, picking up starfish and very gently throwing them into the ocean.

"Young lady," he asked, "Why are you throwing starfish into the ocean?"

"The sun is up, and the tide is going out, and if I do not throw them in they will die."

"But young lady, do you not realize that there are miles and miles of beach and starfish all along it? You cannot possibly make a difference."

The young woman listened politely, paused and then bent down, picked up another starfish and threw it into the sea, past the breaking waves, saying,

"It made a difference for that one."

CHAPTER 5

Sharing Responses

Bringing Family Voices into the Classroom

Dialogue journals provide a venue for sharing both on and off the page. The journals generated dialogue at home as students talked with family members about school, and at school as students shared experiences, perspectives, and understandings from their families. We structured the oral sharing of the journals in the classroom in various ways, depending on the ages and stages of our students—and then restructured sharing as classroom needs evolved. Confronted by classrooms of eager sharers, we found the question was rarely, "Who will share?" It was more often a question of how to create time and a forum for listening to all of those eager to share things such as, "My mom told me that she *hated* reading Shakespeare in high school" or, "This week my brother wrote in my journal because he knows all about machines like we're studying in science." We also recognized that not all families were comfortable writing about all topics, nor were all children comfortable sharing their entries. We worked equally hard at creating an atmosphere of trust for sharing and respect for the decision not to share.

SHARING ROUTINES

Some of us made minor adjustments to our sharing routine. Others chose one structure and later realized a completely different routine would be more effective. We encourage you to experiment with routines to meet the needs of students and teachers as they arise. Below are some of the ways we share in our classrooms.

Morning Meeting

In our elementary classrooms, Morning Meetings (Kriete, 2002) are an integral part of each day. This time of sharing and discussion lends itself well to bringing family voices into the classroom. Sharing during Morning Meeting starts the day positively and builds community. Another benefit to sharing each morning is that it increases motivation for students to return their journals. As classmates share, students without their journals are reminded to bring their journals so they, too, can participate.

In general, our plan was that students who had returned their journals with a message from their families and would like to share had the opportunity during Morning Meeting. Since journals come in on different days, some days only one student shared; other days five students shared. Even if more students volunteered, we rarely had time for more than five a day, so we promised the others that they could share later in the week. On days when we received a large number of journals (usually Mondays), we sometimes also shared at other times of the day.

When students volunteer to share, they read their letter and their family's response, with help from the teacher if needed. Then, the sharer could call on two students to ask questions or make comments relevant to the shared information. This protocol encouraged students to facilitate the discussion, while maintaining a timely flow. The routine also provided practice for students in forming questions and contributing comments to advance conversations, such as making a connection or probing for additional information. For example, Jen's kindergartners shared entries about a book they had read. One student, Michael, asked a classmate, Mack, "Do you like books?" Jen saw a learning opportunity and counseled Mack before he responded.

"That's an important question, Michael," Jen began. "I wonder if we could change it just a little bit, so Mack would have to tell us more than *yes* or *no*?"

Michael grinned, having heard this question posed before, and ventured uncertainly, "Do you like *lots* of books?"

Dahlia raised her hand. "How about, what *kinds* of books do you like?"

"Let's see," Jen said. "Let's have Mack answer that and see what we get!"

Conversations and teachable moments are an integral part of sharing. Teachers and students can learn together how to best discover more about one another's lives. Students learn about one another and can become invested in classmates' goals and interests.

In January, Elyse's 2nd-graders shared their New Year's resolution entries. Tallie explained her goal of biking up a large hill in her neighborhood. Other students gave suggestions, such as starting farther back to pick up speed. Every few weeks, students asked Tallie if she had accomplished her goal. If not, the problem-solving continued with more suggestions, like, "Try standing up while you pump the pedals."

This way of sharing is not exclusively for Morning Meeting. Another segment of the day might work better for some classes, such as a 10-minute gap between recess and lunch or 9 minutes at the end of the day. Teachers who meet with a class for one segment/subject of the day may decide to start or end each class with a few students sharing. Sharing daily as the journals trickle in requires time each day and flexibility that the class and schedule may not allow. Some of us found response groups to work best.

Response Groups

Response groups provide scheduled time for sharing and more time for each student to share, yet they take less class time because sharing is happening simultaneously in groups around the room. As a result, teachers can keep track of who has shared and ensure that each student has quality time to share, especially if some students are pulled out for segments of the day.

Students work in small groups to share and discuss their journal entries. All journals must be turned in the day of sharing for response groups to be most effective. We worked together to develop sharing norms and spent time practicing these norms. For example, we had lessons on how to select the sharing order and how to ask and answer questions. Some of us assigned jobs for each group member, like timekeeper and material manager. Some used a "talking stick" that the speaker held when it was his or her turn to talk. With younger students, small groups work best with a teacher or volunteer in each group.

Response groups are an efficient sharing protocol; however, students and teacher(s) only hear from students in their group. Thus, each student hears fewer perspectives and makes fewer connections to classmates each week. Consequently, teachable moments may not reach the entire class or might be missed altogether. Some of us used response groups when students seemed bored with daily sharing in Morning Meetings, or when we had especially busy weeks and couldn't spare the time for whole-group sharing. It's great to have options and to alternate among them.

Literature Discussions

At the secondary level, Amber invited students to share their family members' entries on Fridays, before they turned in their FDJs. Conversations that stemmed from students' sharing evolved organically, and students made connections to their family members' comments, their own entry, or to the literature that was referenced in the entry. For example, one student would share his mother's entry and reveal to the class why he felt the entry was interesting and worth sharing or how it related to his own response. Another student whose parent said something similar (or totally different) might build off the previous student's sharing, and other class members might pull in examples from the literature to support their classmates' responses. In addition, as Amber and her students continued their exploration of literature, students often referred to family journal entries and to comments about those entries that were made during FDJ discussions. In this way, parents' comments about literature were not only relevant on Friday's, but their voices were consistently integrated into the class's study of literature.

Angela and her 9th-graders also incorporated the sharing of FDJs in their study of literature. She concluded,

> The writing we were doing with poetry during the *Bronx Masquerade* (Grimes, 2002) unit was strong because of their writing in the FDJs. Students shared their poetry in class every Friday during that unit of study, so while they were not always consistently presenting their journals to peers, students were sharing what grew out of their exploration through the readings, journal entries, and poetry. The culture project we completed at the end of the *Bronx Masquerade* unit with our "Where I'm From" (Lyons, 1999) poems, photos from home, and photo narration also grew out of the FDJs.

Students shared these culture projects with their families at an openhouse reception at the end of the year. Thus family members were able to participate in and contribute to the culture project as it developed through the FDJs and enjoy its culmination at the open house.

Evolving Processes

Similar to our Family Dialogue Journal writing processes, our sharing processes evolved with classroom needs and students' input. During their kindergarten year, Jen's class had a consistent sharing routine. From the first journal entry to the last, the children read aloud their letters and their families' responses (with help from Jen) and then called on two friends for questions or comments. When their class looped to 1st grade together and continued journaling, their schedule was different. Some students left the classroom while push-in teachers came to work with small groups. Because Jen felt so strongly that all students should be able to participate in sharing FDJs to build classroom community and extend learning, the class began to consider alternative sharing times to include everyone.

The class voted to do a 1-month trial of small-group sharing. Jen, her student teachers, and any visiting adults present that day divided the children into equal groups before brainstorming or writing their new entry. Each child in the group would then have time to share their journals with one another and to engage in conversation about the journal's contents. Their new sharing routine was quicker, but did not promote the depth of responses Jen desired nor allow for all students to hear from everyone. Further, small-group sharing cut deeply into their FDJ writing time. The children became frustrated when they could not finish their letters before Jen rang the chimes and asked them to turn in their work.

Then, an unfortunate event made clear to Jen that it was time to think of an alternative to this routine. As the class sat down in a circle to read their journals aloud, Jen's student teacher informed her that Jen had not yet taped the translation of the Spanish-speaking families' responses to this week's entry as she usually did each week. Jen sighed deeply. She had completely forgotten. Mr. Oswaldo had sent her his translations, and she failed to copy and cut them out for the journals. So, she did the only thing she could think to do: Jen split the class based on the language in which their family had written their journal response and asked Mr. Oswaldo if he could read with those children whose responses were in Spanish. She read with the students whose families wrote in English.

Jen felt that this segmented their class in ways to which they were not accustomed. She wanted to minimize the likelihood of separating the class like this and worried that small groups may not be the best strategy for her classroom. Therefore, after consulting with the students, Jen's class circled back around to the option of sharing during Morning Meeting. There were still time constraints, since other teachers arrived for support early in the day, but Jen realized they had 15 minutes between recess and their specials (e.g., PE, music, art) block that they could use to finish sharing and commenting on journals if needed.

For Jen's classroom, sharing FDJs needed to include the rich, unique perspectives of all students and families. There was no substitute for being present as every child read aloud, since no one could know who in the class might make a meaningful connection or ask a probing question for anyone else's journal. Their voices were equally important, meant for all community members to hear, and Jen committed herself to sharing time that honored this belief.

We encourage readers to experiment with sharing protocols to find a system that works well for your students and class schedule. Bringing families' voices out of the FDJs and into the classroom discourse is important whether you share a few journals each day, split into small groups for discussions, or develop another way to share. Although it can be difficult to fit a sharing routine into every classroom schedule, sharing has many benefits to students, both socially and academically. Understanding why sharing is important may help to keep sharing a priority in your classroom's FDJ process.

Sharing consistently was difficult in Angela's 9th-grade classroom because they were limited by the 55-minute class period. When they had time at the beginning of class, Angela passed the journals back to students as they came in the room so that they could look at them until the tardy bell rang. They read what they'd written, what their parents had written, and Angela's response. They could then swap journals or talk in groups of two or three people around their seats depending on how much time they had. On days when she had enough time, Angela then brought the class together and students reported on what they had shared with their neighboring classmates.

Some days Angela saved this sharing process for the end of class and dedicated a larger chunk of time so they could generate their next set of topics once sharing time ended. Angela noted,

> Having the students sitting in groups during sharing time definitely lent itself to more discussion. I structured groups frequently with the two pieces of literature we used the FDJs with, *Bronx Masquerade* (Grimes, 2002) and *They Poured Fire on Us from the Sky* (Deng et al., 2005). It was easier to incorporate the FDJs into their groups because they knew groups were used to discussing and generating ideas. So when we turned to the whole class focus after sharing in our small groups, they seemed to have more to share with all of us.

Based on the feedback Angela got from parents and students, some wanted to share more frequently. Camilla's mom wrote on the survey that she felt the students should have more time to talk about the responses in their journals. She wanted to see them making more connections across the classroom. Angela reflected on how to best incorporate more time for sharing the FDJs.

> Being that this was my first experience using the journals, I think I was overjoyed at getting responses and that the students were mostly buying in to the whole idea. I had not really gotten beyond worrying if they would reject them altogether to think more closely about how to fully integrate sharing them into the fabric of our weekly schedule.

WHY SHARE?

The written dialogue is reason enough to pursue FDJs with students and families; orally sharing the journals makes the process even more meaningful. Together, written and verbal sharing create personally relevant academic conversations where all parties can learn about and from one another. In the process, students are able to practice respectful listening and speaking protocols.

Imagine a student shares how his mother uses measurement to cook their family's favorite dish. The class is able to review measurement with a real-world example. Perhaps the class has been learning to measure distance; now the conversation has led them to consider how to measure liquids and solids. Students may make connections to measuring boards for building a community chicken coop in their mobile home park, to estimating the distance the family travels to Mexico to visit family, or to measuring the distance between rows for different kinds of crops. This could lead to a class project related to science or health that involves families, such as by the class inviting parents to teach them about laying out a garden at the school.

We share FDJs in our classrooms for many reasons. Although we label our examples with a specific reason for sharing—family voices in the classroom, building community, and more complete understandings—we hope you see the numerous benefits interwoven throughout each classroom snapshot.

Hearing Family Voices in the Classroom

Families' perspectives are powerful influences in learning content and learning about one another, and FDJs bring those families' voices into the classroom conversations. Amber's class provides a good example. Lana, a student Amber admired for her bold and quirky sense of style in both clothes and writing, shared her father's response regarding events in Egypt. First, Lana gave the class some background on her father: "He is from Lebanon, a country close in proximity to Egypt, and he speaks six languages." Lana said that her father had related a class reading, *La Revolution Francaise,* to recent events in Egypt. He wrote:

> The French society underwent epic transformations as feudal, aristocratic, and religious privileges evaporated under a sustained assault from the masses on the streets. Old ideas about hierarchy and tradition succumbed to new principles of citizenship and inalienable rights. The Egyptians are most likely hoping for a similar outcome— aspirations for social, political, and economic rights.

Lana's classmates were impressed that her father could read in French, let alone speak five other languages. Lana smiled at the reaction of her classmates and told them more about the other languages her father spoke. As she shared her father's perspective and interesting facts about his life, Lana experienced open respect and appreciation for her parent by her peers, something that does not happen often in high school classroom conversation.

Shortly thereafter, Lana's father responded to a prompt asking about a time he felt a racial, religious, ethnic, or cultural difference. He wrote:

> When I first arrived at [city] to go to college, I did not speak hardly any English. And, what little I knew and spoke came out with a heavy accent. [The college] was a beautiful place with decent people. But they were very suspicious of nonlocals and considered most strangers as "foreigners." The constant questioning of "where are you from, boy" or "you ain't from around here, are you" made me feel like I was an alien from outer space and made it difficult, initially, to fit in and make friends. As I got better command of the English language, began adopting some of the colloquialisms, and gained a better understanding of the local subculture, things got better. I began to feel more comfortable and accepted.

In recounting his first years in the United States, Lana's father noted that his ability with languages was a hindrance rather than a valued form of cultural capital. Amber believes that Lana shared with her father the class's awe and amazement when she told them about his linguistic abilities, creating a space for him to write about how the reaction to being able to speak Arabic, Lebanese, French, Egyptian, and Saudi was not always valued because he had an accent when speaking English.

Building Community

Sharing conversations like the one Amber's class had about language prejudice allows members of the classroom community to understand one another better and make connections, which contributes to a positive classroom community. Stephanie's class realized a special connection that many students and parents in their class shared after writing home about September 11, 2001. Through discussing this historic day, it became clear that Stephanie's students knew little about the event. Some students knew that the day was related to some really tall buildings called the Twin Towers and a couple knew they were knocked down.

The class became engaged in the topic, asking questions and wanting to know more, so they utilized their FDJs to extend this conversation at home. KenAsia asked, "Do you remember when the Twin Towers fell down? Was I born yet?" Treasure wrote,

> Dear mom and dad, this week in third grade we talk about conflict and change like the twin towers. Some jets crash into the twin towers. That was the conflict and the change was people had to help.

As children brought the journals to school the following week, Stephanie noticed several common threads among almost all the journals. Most of their mothers wrote about being at home and watching the news on television. Then, the class realized a strong connection. One mother wrote,

> On 9/11/2001, your brother Daniel was 7 months old and I was pregnant with you, I remember waking up and the footage was on every channel on the TV. Only the first airplane had gone into one of the Twin Towers. Everyone was terribly sad. But the worst part was actually watching live footage of the 2nd airplane crashing into the other tower.

Another mother responded,

> On September 11, 2001, I was pregnant with you, I remember I woke up late that morning, went to the kitchen to get something to eat,

turned on the TV and what I saw was a huge building falling down, so I decided not to see news and I changed the channel and it was the same building falling down, then I started to pay attention on what they were saying. This is one of the worst tragedies of the U.S.

Their mothers were pregnant with them on or around September 11. Sharing allowed students to discover this commonality. Their families' perspectives allowed them to understand what occurred and what their parents experienced as a result of the events on September 11, a significant American event that occurred early in their lives or, for most in Stephanie's class, prior to their births.

Developing More Complete Understanding

Families' contributions can provide new perspectives to consider, allowing everyone to broaden their understandings of a topic, of people, and of the world. Students often communicated information beyond the written journal entries to provide more complete pictures. Elliot, a student many in Amber's class would define as the class clown, always turned in a journal that contained very short entries from his mother. At first, Amber attributed this to Elliot not giving his mother enough time to complete the journal entry. Amber imagined Elliot, happy-go-lucky and impulsive, throwing it at his mother Sunday night or Monday morning and saying, "Here, write in this really quick. It's due today." Another teacher might have interpreted the clipped responses as lack of interest on the mother's part.

Hoping to gain some insight, Amber asked Elliot if he would like to share his entry for the week. Before reading or discussing the contents of the journal, Elliot explained that his mom had just flown in from another state and that she had bought *Animal Farm*, the book he was reading, at the airport to read on the plane so that she could talk to him about it when she got home. After some probing, Amber learned that, as a single parent, Elliot's mother traveled often, leaving his older brother in charge of the household until she got back.

Because of the conversation that stemmed from the sharing ritual, Amber learned that neither of her imagined scenarios was true. Elliot's mother responded quickly and efficiently to the prompts because she had limited time at home and wanted to spend that time talking to her son, not writing in a journal. As Elliot's case demonstrated, the information or context provided about students' parents during sharing helped Amber understand that Elliot's mother was very much interested in her son's academic success, so much so that she engaged herself in her son's assignment by reading the book he chose. She is very much involved in his education, even if it was not obvious through the FDJ alone. Elliot's explanation during FDJ sharing provided a more complete understanding of his mother's ideas about the weekly topic and his family's unique circumstances, things that would have been missed with only the written journal entries.

MAKE YOUR PURPOSES KNOWN

Each of us developed and refined our reasons as well as rituals for sharing, but it was equally important for students and families to understand the importance. Some of us explained our reasons for sharing the journals with students and families; others developed or discovered our purposes together as a learning community.

Jennifer's class realized the importance of sharing their FDJs together one Wednesday morning. The previous week's entry had been,

> This week we have been learning about pumpkins. We made a pumpkin faces graph, we counted pumpkin seeds, and we did a pumpkin activity. When you were little did you do any of those?

Elizabeth, a student in Jennifer's class, read her dad's response:

> Where I grow up we don't do any of those activities because the Halloween tradition is not strong as is here in the United States. And the pumpkins are not a popular item, you barely find them in the stores. At this time of the year everybody is more interested in pay a visit to the cemetery to remember the love ones that passed away, and everybody is shopping for flowers and decorations for the places where they rest in peace.

The class clapped and prepared for the next student to share. Jennifer paused, realizing just how valuable families' experiences and perspectives were. She wanted her classroom community to appreciate and take advantage of how much they could learn from one another. So instead of moving on to the next student, Jennifer asked,

> "What have we learned about Elizabeth's dad?"

Hands enthusiastically rose around the circle and bodies sat up a little bit straighter. Students made comparisons to their own lives, such as, "Her dad didn't do pumpkin activities when he was little like we have." They asked questions about visiting the cemetery and learned from those in the class who celebrated Dia de los Muertos (Day of the Dead) about gathering to pray for and remember those who had died.

Other students made inferences, such as, "Her dad is from somewhere else," giving Elizabeth a chance to talk about her dad's native country.

Jennifer was excited that her students had been listening to each other. They enjoyed sharing their families' responses and embraced the discussions that the responses generated. With each journal shared that week, Jennifer encouraged a brief conversation about what they could learn from the response.

By Friday, the class had discovered that their families had many different experiences with Halloween and Dia de los Muertos. During their morning meeting, the class talked about how their families are from all over the world. Jennifer illustrated this by asking, "Whose family is from Honduras?" A few hands went up. "El Salvador?" A few more hands. "Korea?" One hand. "Mexico?" A bunch of hands. Jennifer highlighted how their families' knowledge and experiences had taught them about holidays in a different and more interesting way than a school book. The class discussed how their families had taught them that Halloween is not celebrated all around the world.

Jennifer decided to extend the Morning Meeting conversations into the FDJs. The students wrote to their families about how they had learned through the FDJs about one another's families. Then they asked their families, "What do you want my class to know about our family?" This question brought the importance of learning from families to the front and center of their conversations the following week as students shared responses. Maria's family wrote:

> I am happy that you are learning. One thing that I want your class to know about our family is that we are Mexican. We are a family of five: you, me, your dad, brother, sister, and of course our dog, Lacey. We have been here in the U.S. for about 10 plus years. Both of your parents work. We want for our kids to achieve everything they want to achieve.

Jazmin's mom responded:

> I want you to know that we are a very close family and that we love you and you are our life and we hope God blesses you and keep you for all the days of your life continue giving your intelligence so that you can become an important person I love you very much. (translated from Spanish)

Elizabeth read her family's response: "We are a small family is just 3 of us we loved when mom and dad have the weekend off to do things together we enjoy movies and tv show together."

Alejandro's older sister wrote, "It is pretty interesting that you are learning about families. I hope that you tell your class about our family, and I hope you learn about other student families."

Jennifer and her class openly discussed the importance of respecting family contributions and perspectives to help them better understand their classmates and community. They invited families to contribute to the conversation, and they discovered together the value of sharing various viewpoints and learning from others.

Part of respecting families is respecting their privacy and their own purposes for engaging—or declining to engage—in the FDJs. While students' and families' rights to privacy must be respected, there are ways to avoid situations and entries that may prove uncomfortable for students. Amber talked with her students, emphasizing that this journal was not a diary: It is not for "your eyes only." She encouraged students not to write anything in the journal that they did not want her or their parents to read. Amber stressed that while this type of expression is important, the FDJ was not the venue for such writing. "I tell them that I care deeply for them and hope that they can come to me, face to face or through a personal note, if they need help, support, or advice with any issue, serious or trivial." However, she asked them to reserve their FDJs for relating their experiences to the classroom curriculum. As examples in this book illustrate, journal discussions were centered around curriculum. While many responses were indeed personal, keeping the journal based on what is being studied defines the journal as an academic narrative that allows for personal reflection, not vice versa.

Discovering the purposes for sharing family responses can be a powerful venture. You might investigate your purpose directly, like Jennifer's class, or your reasons for sharing may unfold throughout the year—and might unfold differently from year to year. A major purpose that we will delve into in more detail in the next chapter is creating dynamic, critical curriculum that incorporates family funds of knowledge.

CHAPTER 6

Creating Connectional and Critical Curriculum

In this chapter we discuss what we learned from families and how family funds of knowledge (Gonzáles, Moll, & Amanti, 2005) became central to our curriculum. This is what we call creating a *connectional curriculum*, practices that link classroom learning with families and communities (Allen, 2007). We are not referring to parents helping with a sheet of math homework or signing agendas or reading logs. Connectional curriculum grows out of what we learn from families about their experiences, jobs, histories, and opinions, as we illustrate in this chapter.

In addition, many of us began using FDJs in our classrooms because we sought a *critical curriculum*, one in which dialogue supports the questioning of dominant cultural practices that oppress others while encouraging social action (Darder, Baltodano, & Torres, 2009). We had in common years of Red Clay Writing Project (RCWP) experiences of discussing the power and privilege differentials students and families experience based on race, social class, gender, and other cultural constructs. Central to all our shared activities in RCWP is the following RCWP tenet:

> We see literacy as deeply integral to developing teaching/learning relationships that addresses *issues of educational equity and social justice.* Using this critical lens helps us think about how to prepare students to participate as citizens working towards a truly democratic society. As the United States grows more diverse, issues of language, literacy, and culture become increasingly critical. Living by democratic principles has become more complicated and threatened in recent years, and the existential, political, and social needs for literacy have grown geometrically, especially for those students disenfranchised from the mainstream. We view literacy not only as a tool for learning or means of enjoyment, but also as a way to actively participate in and shape a democracy.

As critical educators, we believed that including families in discussion through Family Dialogue Journals would encourage students and families

84

to question the world and even their own ideologies. Therefore, many of the journal entries invited students, families, and us to reflect on social issues and inequities. In the following sections we offer examples of how we moved towards a connectional and critical curriculum, one that incorporated family funds of knowledge and that engaged students, families, and teachers in critique of society, education, and our lives.

INCORPORATING FAMILY FUNDS OF KNOWLEDGE

The primary purpose of the Family Dialogue Journals was to incorporate students' home lives into the classroom. Weaving family funds of knowledge into the curriculum not only created a bridge between in-school and out-of-school lives; it also validated students' household knowledge and ways of learning. We tried to incorporate families' funds of knowledge into the classroom in various ways. Often, this depended on the grade level and subject matter being discussed. In this section we show how Elyse, Stephanie, and Jen incorporated funds of knowledge into their elementary school classes differently from how Amber, a high school teacher, integrated them into her classroom. Despite the difference, the value of family knowledge resulted in a more dynamic curriculum and supported student learning.

Using Family Knowledge to Build Community

One of Stephanie's favorite ways to build community in her classroom at the beginning of each year was to engage in a study of names. She read aloud *The Old Woman Who Named Things* (Rylant, 2000), *The Name Jar* (Choi, 2003), and *Chrysanthemum* (Henkes, 2008) to begin their inquiry about names. This usually made the students wonder where their names originated; naming is often linked to family histories and social networks. So in their journals they told their families about the stories they had been reading and asked them, "How did you choose my name?" Because the students were dying to know the answer and were equally excited to share their name story, the Morning Meeting sharing of this entry was particularly engaging and helped to lay a foundation for sharing all year.

Olivia's parents told her that her name "came from an old lady at the nursing home your Granny worked at." Treasure's mom responded:

> When it was time to name you, I searched and searched for the perfect name. I wanted your name to be so unique that no one else would have that name. So, I picked Treasure for your name. It was a one-of-a-kind name, and it described what you are to me . . . my Treasure!

Stephanie also had one student, Alisa, who spelled her name differently from what was on the school roster. Despite the fact that she knew Alisa was a strong reader, Stephanie thought initially that she was misspelling her name. Alisa emigrated from Mexico and when she came to public school in America, her mom decided to change the spelling of her original name, Asalia, to the "American" spelling, Alisa. Through the name-story entry in the family journals, Stephanie realized that this student did know how to spell her name, she was just spelling it the way her mother spelled it at home as opposed to the school spelling. From that point on, Stephanie made a conscious effort to spell her name the way she and her mother spelled it. Another student's mother emphasized the apostrophe that she placed in her daughter's name and while many of the school records left out the apostrophe in D'Nisha, because of the entry from her mother, Stephanie made sure to include the apostrophe.

In this way, the journals gave Stephanie valuable knowledge, not only about her students' writing abilities early in the year, but also about their preferences with regard to their names. The journal dialogue ensured that the most important proper noun in the English language—one's name—was spelled and pronounced correctly and linked those names to family stories, traditions, and relationships.

Connecting Curriculum to FDJ Entries

As winter warmed into spring, Elyse's kindergarten class asked their families, "Why do you like spring?" Several families responded about spending time outside, and a few families responded about the gardens they were planting. The students beamed with connections, realizing that they, too, loved going to the lake or helping their mom or dad plant flowers and vegetables. The following week, the class focused on nutrition. As students identified and named healthy food choices, Elyse connected the class discussion to the vegetables mentioned in journals the previous week, making the subject matter more personally relevant and memorable.

Connecting journal conversations to new classroom content evolved from a practice that the teacher modeled into a student norm. The following journal entry told about the flowers students had planted in the classroom. The students talked about what their plants needed and asked, "What do you need?" Parents wrote about a variety of needs, such as water, food, and love. As the class began their living and nonliving science unit, students eagerly called out connections. "We wrote about that!" "Like our plants." "My mom needs water [to live]." Students began to reference their journal entries and family responses when they were relevant to class discussions.

In Jennifer's 2nd grade, they were studying temperature. Elizabeth's dad noticed that she was watching the weather news at home. Elizabeth wrote,

We have been Leaning about temperature. Do you have a thermometer?

Elizabeth: I saw you Paying attention to the TV the Past few Days and watching close all the temperature in the weather News

- We do Have thermomoters at home as a matter of fact we Have a few diferent kinds
- We Have one that we use for you when you are sick to make sure you don't Have fever.
- We Have one that measure the temperature in the House
- and we Have the ones Daddy use in His Job

Love always,
Daddy

Family Dialogue Journals also served as a way to inform teachers about students' academic interests and led to the creation of new projects or altered curriculum. For example, in January, one of Stephanie's new students, J'Don, really enjoyed the science unit about heat, especially heat produced from the sun. In his journal he asked his dad, "Did you learn about the sun as a kid?" His father replied, "I also learned about the sun when I was in school. I learned that the sun is a star and other stars that we see in the sky at night are also other suns in other galaxies." J'Don became even more interested in learning about the sun after his father's response. After he shared the entry during Morning Meeting, the other students also volunteered information they knew concerning the sun and surrounding planets. This discussion enraptured the class in a 30-minute

---

FDJ ENTRIES ON ESTABLISHED CLASSROOM CURRICULUM

- What do you predict I will be when I grow up? (Elyse's classroom)
- What do you know about/how do you celebrate Earth Day? (Elyse's classroom)
- When is satire appropriate, and when is it offensive? (Amber's classroom)
- Can you show me how you would solve 59 divided by 4? (Stephanie's classroom)
- Where on the map did your family stories take place? (Jen's classroom)
- Have you ever written poetry? (Jennifer's classroom)
- What do you remember us learning about over the past year or 2 years? (Jen's classroom)

discussion with the students asking questions and sharing their own and their families' knowledge about the sun.

This discussion led them to a science inquiry project that allowed the students to practice their research inquiry and writing skills. They all completed a solar system project that they researched, designed, and presented to the class. This project originated because families shared their knowledge in the journals. How often do we miss opportunities to bring in family knowledge to shape and enrich our curriculum?

Student and parent responses also inspired Amber to alter her curriculum, sometimes immediately, to capitalize on students' interests and, at other times, to address more drastic changes for the next semester or even the next year. In some cases, family entries inspired her to create a new lesson or project. In other instances, the information in the journals made Amber reassess major elements of her curriculum, such as the novels that the class would read the following year. In both cases, the dialogue between the student, family, and Amber influenced her instructional practices, bringing the family permanently into her classroom as they helped build her instructional calendar.

One assignment in Amber's classroom that sprang from the dialogue in the FDJs revolved around formal language versus street or slang language. The students wanted to write about their favorite slang words, which morphed into a question about favorite slang, dialect, and academic words. So, capitalizing on their excitement, Amber transitioned into the next unit, *Othello*, by having students experiment with using Shakespearian slang and proper Elizabethan language, showing how language has been coded since before the 1600s. Using a list of words to insult an enemy, Amber's students reveled in calling each other "fobby beef-witted harpies" and "gorbellied onion-eyed hugger-muggers." Next, students tried to translate Shakespearian slang into the slang that they would use today. Amber then gave them a list of words that were used in formal Elizabethan language, and students translated modern sentences into Shakespearian sentences, focusing on *thee* and *thou* and *wither* and *whilst*, and so on. Then students talked about situations in the play where slang or formal language would be used and by whom. This led to a discussion about the power of language and how Shakespeare used language registers to identify the class of a character. Amber changed the introduction to her Shakespeare unit to take advantage of the interests her students conveyed in their FDJs.

Amber also found that the FDJs helped her make long-term changes to her curriculum. At the end of the first semester, Amber asked students to assess their progress in the course and share what they would like to see changed. Many students shared what they perceived as weaknesses in their language arts skills, and parents also mentioned places where they thought their child could improve. For example, after pointing out his strengths, Rajak's mother wrote that he "needs to get more organized and work on his analytical skills," while Rajak felt that his weakness was "time management while taking multiple choice tests" like the timed, multiple-choice AP exam. By attending to his anxiety, Amber was able to alleviate Rajak's fears and, as it turned out, the anxiety of many of the other students, by working in some timed, multiple-choice practice sessions. Furthermore, Amber assured his mother that students would continue analyzing literature and language and practice organizing ideas for essays.

Students were also able to share in the FDJs what they enjoyed most about the class and advocate for changes they would like to see in the course. Casey, a quiet baseball player, wrote, "My favorite part of this class is the group activities . . . listening to others' viewpoints helps me to greater understand certain ideas about a subject." His mother, an elementary school teacher, responded, "Group discussions and activities are definitely more effective in the classroom . . . this is also a great way to prepare these kids for what lies ahead in college." Kelly, a student who was passionate about environmental and women's rights issues, asked if students could bring in an essay for the class to read and discuss. She wrote, "We could use past issues, such as women's rights, and compare that to what society (writers) view now . . . that would be quite a discussion." A quiet girl who would not have made this request to Amber in person, Kelly was able to express her request through the FDJ, a democratic tool that allowed all voices to be heard. Amber wondered, when was the last time parents felt like they had a voice in the construction of curriculum? Through the FDJs, Amber was able to construct the next semester's curriculum based on communication among students, parents, and teachers.

One curricular change Amber made was from what she saw missing in FDJ conversations. As she read student and parent entries visciously attacking stereotyping because of race or sex, Amber noted that students seemed comfortable with stereotypes of people affected by poverty. This was revealed in their responses regarding social class to William Faulkner's *As I Lay Dying* (1930/1985). Because of her students' lack of experience with financial need, Amber decided to add another novel to the curriculum, *Angela's Ashes* by Frank McCourt (1996), hoping that her students could read about someone's personal experiences living in poverty. In addition, she added *Nickel and Dimed* by Barbara Ehrenreich (2002) to her summer reading list, preparing students for the issues of social class that would be addressed in her class throughout the year.

With more to teach in less time, teachers feel constant pressure. Some feel that to cover all the standards before testing they become like a farmer feeding chickens, tossing the feed out in hopes the chickens will get what they need. Freire (1970) referred to this attempt to "deposit" knowledge as "banking education." He advocated a "problem posing" approach, an inquiry stance in which learners actively engage in posing and investigating questions about topics, questions that spring from classroom topics—but that may not be directly related to the original topic. Family Dialogue

FDJ Questions from Students Leading to Inquiry-Based Curriculum

- Who has been a role model in your life? (Elyse's classroom)
- What things are accepted in your culture that might not be accepted in another? Explain what it was like to come to this realization. (Angela's classroom)
- How would you choose to save an ice cube? (Stephanie's classroom)
- Do you remember when the Twin Towers fell down? Was I born yet? (Stephanie's classroom)
- When do you see people who look different from you in the world? (Jen's classroom)

Journals allow students, parents, and teachers to engage actively as they question and reason together. Inquiry has the power to transform a list of learning objectives into powerful topics of discussion and negotiation. As we participated in a more inquiry-based approach in our classrooms, we found that because students are learning and understanding at a deeper level as they engage with the journals and their family members, there *is* actually enough time to fit it all in. More importantly, our students retained the knowledge much better because of the active role they played in questioning, inquiring, and learning.

Building on Cultural and Linguistic Diversity

Family Dialogue Journals brought curricular content to life in our classrooms as we integrated family connections. Often, this integration began with a topic a student offered as a possible focus for FDJs. Students deepened their understanding of language arts in all our classrooms, as well as of math, social studies, and science standards in elementary classrooms, by linking learning to family responses and perspectives. This created a dialogic curriculum based on the cultural diversity in our classroom.

Jen and her young students identified one particularly strong connection between curricular content and families' backgrounds, which led to an investigation of families' geographic history.

"So," Jen began, after she and her students settled in to their carpet squares, "What do you think you want to write to our families this week?"

Students' hands shot up in the air, and they began discussing options. Some children were interested in asking families about maps. Others wanted to inquire about where their relatives lived. Still others had an interest in talking to families about their location in the world, which the children had begun studying by creating a diorama displaying the way a neighborhood fits into a city, a city fits into a state, and a state fits into a country. Each of these options was directly connected to the 1st-grade standards, and the children's ideas for journal dialogue made clear they were interested in learning this information as it related to their families' backgrounds.

Jen saw an opportunity to merge these topics. "What do you think about asking your families about the place on a map where your families' stories took place?" she asked. The term "family stories" conjured up communal images for the children; during the previous year, they and their families had coauthored a book of personal narratives that focused on family events that were important to them. Jen also asked if the children would like to place pins on a map of North America as their families wrote back, offering a visual to aid in the students' understanding of maps.

The children voted to accept this idea as their next family dialogue journal entry. Then, they spread out around the room, some with clipboards on pillows and others scooted up to rectangular tables, and wrote about the place where their favorite family stories happened.

Some children, including Hector, wrote about Mexico. "My mom and dad live in Mexico, he wrote, but I don't live in Mexico." This journal entry was an opportunity for him to acknowledge the differences between his upbringing and that of his parents, while at the same time connecting this place to what he was learning about maps. "You get lots [lost], you ned [need] a map," he reminded his family. Mack wrote about his vacation to Florida, telling his family, "Flrdu was r family srey. Fudu was far away sed Mack. [Florida was our family story. Florida was far away said Mack."]

The students finished each letter with, "¿De dónde proceden nuestros familias?/Where do our family stories come from on a map?" Then they placed their journals in book bags and carried them home.

When the journals trickled in on Monday morning, Jen and her students read them aloud during Morning Meeting. Jen's coteacher translated Spanish entries to English, and four children read aloud their original entry, along with each family's response. They learned that Mack's family had lived in the town in which their school sat for generations, and Mack proudly placed a pin with his name attached to it on the class's map of North America. They compared this to the second pin he placed on Florida, a place he and his family often vacationed. The class talked about how Mack knew it was far away, but looked much closer on the map. When Hector placed a pin on Michoacán, Mexico, Jen and her students discussed its distance from the other pins, as well as his mother's response regarding the differences in language, dress, and meals between Mexico and the United States. Other children who placed a family pin on Mexico agreed with this and shared what they knew about the brightly colored clothing, meals of beans and tortillas, and holidays like Día de los Muertos (Day of the Dead), which their families had described to them.

The map of North America remained on the wall at the front of their classroom for the rest of the year, with students referring to it in their writing and sharing its meaning with visitors. Some students began studying a globe every morning, comparing what they saw there to what they had posted on the wall, oftentimes identifying the place representing their families' history. In these ways, Jen's class used the information in the FDJs and the classroom dialogue that had been made possible by the journals to make abstract concepts from the 1st-grade standards more concrete. The cultural diversity in her classroom made this deep understanding of geography tangible.

Linguistic diversity was also a resource in each of our classrooms, from Jennifer's multiple nationalities and languages to classrooms with multiple English dialects to several classrooms where Spanish was the predominant home language, such as Jen's.

Jen and her students began the Family Dialogue Journals the first Friday of the school year. After coconstructing their letter about "1st-grade hopes and dreams," Jen handed out new black-and-white composition notebooks. Students spread out around the room. The possibilities inherent in the blank pages of new journals seemed to refuel the children, tired out by their first full week back at school, and soon they were writing at desks, on pillows, or under tables with friends.

Jen and her student teacher rotated around the room, conferencing with and refocusing students as needed on the question to the children's families: "What are your hopes and dreams for me this year?" She stopped to write "¿Cuales son sus sueños y esperanzas para mí?" in Naldo's journal, as his family primarily spoke Spanish. Naldo's writing already consisted of multiple sentences. Jen's eyes widened when she realized he was writing his entry entirely in Spanish! He was a fearless speller, stretching out the sounds he heard and proudly displaying "keyro" as his sound-spelled version of "quiero," as he wrote that his hope for the year was to learn to drive a car.

Naldo shared his biliterate venture: "My mom wants me to learn Spanish and English this year. She will teach me to read in Spanish and I will teach her English, because she doesn't know much English yet and she wants me to help her learn." Jen was both surprised and impressed by his linguistic risk-taking. However, it seemed to Naldo to be a natural extension of his growing mastery of sounds. Why wouldn't he be writing in Spanish, since his family spoke Spanish at home, and he was going to place this journal in his book bag to share with them? He knew his audience!

Jen wondered what inspired Naldo to write this entry in Spanish. Was it the fact that they always translated their journal's question to Spanish, and this was a natural extension? Was it because their FDJs had inspired Jen and her students to discuss how they could learn from and with their families? Or was it, as Naldo explained, fueled by the deal his mother struck with him, promising she would assist him in learning to read Spanish if he did the same for her with English?

More than likely, it was a combination of these factors. Jen made a commitment to highlight Naldo's entry during Morning Meeting share time and to encourage other students to write to families in *their* home language, as well. Naldo's connection between his journal's language and his audience helped Jen to realize writing in home languages was a powerful way to share families' funds of knowledge (González, Moll, & Amanti, 2005).

In Amber's AP English class, a class-generated prompt about language registers allowed students to discuss language diversity when sharing their journal responses. This prompt also created a venue for students to express how they felt about their own linguistic register: Southern vernacular. While most students were fluent in the power language of Standard English as well as street slang, they also participated in a linguistically diverse community because of the region in which they lived. Josh wrote, "I say ain't, y'all, and yonder a lot. I have just heard those words and other Southern phrases so much of my life; they have just been ingrained into my vocabulary." His mother included some Southern idioms and maxims as well.

Kelly wrote, "I use y'all, which I'm not sure is even a word." Another student said that "these terms have changed with time as more and more people become lazy and choose not to use the complete word." Clearly, students saw Southern vernacular as "bad" English, not realizing that there are rules that govern such speech. This discussion, which occurred due to the FDJ prompt, lead to a mini-lesson on how "y'all" is a contraction of "you all" and how to spell it correctly. Amber also told students the rule of dropping the *g* on words and replacing *w* with *er* was also a consistent marker within the dialect. By discussing how Southern vernacular had "rules" just like Standard English, it was Amber's hope that it validated their use of such language. Furthermore, it made them more receptive to understanding that other dialects such as African American Vernacular were rule-based dialects that marked individuals as a part of a community. Building curriculum that is grounded in the cultural and linguistic diversity of students and families is radical and often empowering, but it is not sufficient. We must also develop critical ways of examining the world and our places in it (Freire, 2005).

DEVELOPING CRITICAL LENSES

As students read, view, or write texts, critical educators equip them to question and evaluate, pushing toward the deepest levels of comprehension, including critiques of privilege. Students discuss power structures related to issues that directly affect them, their families, and their communities: race, social class, gender, language, religion, family structures, ability, and many other cultural influences. One of our goals in using FDJs was to help students develop a critical lens through their written questions, their familial dialogue at home, and through their discussions in the classroom. Sometimes this was challenging, as we wanted the topics to come from what the students identified to write about. How does one write a question about counting back change in math that is thought provoking and geared toward social justice? During certain weeks, a critical question was just not possible, and other weeks, students blew us away with the scope of their thought processes. At other times, the nature of a student's or parent's entry presented teachers with an opportunity to engage the class in critical discussion. However, as Amber will share, not all critical questions necessarily led to a desired critical response.

Developing the Critical Question

Sometimes students developed critical questions. Allen, a new student, moved into Stephanie's classroom mid-year; he was the only White child in the class. One day, when Stephanie asked him to partner with another student, Allen responded, "Me and my daddy don't really like Black people." Stephanie decided that exploring perspectives on race through children's literature might help Allen. She read aloud *The Other Side* by Jacqueline Woodson (2001). They talked about the struggles that the main characters, one Black, one White, faced during segregation, ways the girls and their mothers helped to "knock down the fence" of segregation, and how the class could do the same. By Friday the students were still fixated on the fence metaphor; in the journals students told their parents about how the girls helped to end segregation by being friends even though they were different races. The students then posed the question, "How have you been affected by segregation? What have you done to knock down the fence?"

Many students shared experiences from their grandparents' childhood about segregated schools or how a relative had a friend of a different race growing up. One boy shared, "I wanted to play baseball but other White boys were already playing. They offered for me to play too. We knocked down a fence that day." Allen didn't share anything, but he checked out *The Other Side* from the library. Stephanie asked, "What book did you check out Allen?" He held the book up and responded, "I'm going to take it home to read with my dad." He began knocking down a fence that day.

Not all critical questions come so easily. Jennifer's school was hosting a bake sale to benefit their Relay for Life team. Her class created a rap, which they performed on the morning announcements. This was the highlight of their week and the students had no problem constructing the body of the letter, but the question stumped them. Students suggested questions like, "When you were little did you go on the announcements?" and "Tell me about a time you wrote a rap." Jennifer tried to help students generate critical dialogue.

She said, "Think about what we were promoting."

Students answered, "A bake sale!" "Brownies!" "Food!"

She tried again, "But think about who was doing the bake sale. It was Relay for Life, right? What is Relay for Life?"

They answered, "People who help other people!"

"Exactly! Maybe we could steer our question towards people helping people!" They decided to ask, "Tell me about a time you helped someone."

Jennifer and her students found out that one student's brother had raised money to help the homeless, and another mom donated money to an organization. Elizabeth's dad said, "We helped people every year when during Thanksgiving I cook dinner for a shelter in downtown Atlanta, and also we donate clothes and toys to the local charity store." Looking back, Jennifer regretted not extending the questioning to promote critical thinking that related to their own lives and perceptions about the world around them.

Later that year, after studying Rosa Parks and the Civil Rights Movement, students wanted to write about this pivotal time. They decided to ask their families, "What would you boycott for?" Some of their families would boycott for things like human rights and being "kicked out of my job unfairly," while others said they might not boycott, were unsure, or were "really not in favor of boycott. I won't do it, I will find a different way to solve my problem."

Developing Critical Thinking

Angela noticed that it took her students several rounds of responding in the FDJs, talking and writing with families, and sharing family responses in class to look at texts with a critical lens and raise questions that might elicit a critical response. One of the first students to make this shift was Alexis when she focused on a question considering society's perceptions of beauty.

Alexis: I think society's ideal look is what we see in the magazines and movies. Skinny white girls who looks like they don't eat anything. I think the media or entertainment has brainwashed us. And I think that's really why a lot of people go bulimic and anorexic, because they feel like they have to look like the girls in the magazines and truth be told those girls don't even look like that. Society's look just isn't ideal.

Alexis's mother: I agree with you about what society thinks we should look like. We all are different shapes, color, and cultures. We should want people to love their differences. Everyone don't look the same. Society doesn't decide how we should feel about ourselves. We should decide that.

Angela: I agree. We get messages that there is only a limited way to be, but if we look around we see many who don't match that "look."

Beauty comes from within. That was one thing that my mother always said to me, but it is difficult to find that value in magazines and movies.

In this entry, Alexis questioned society's standard of beauty and compared it to the actual composition of society, most of which does not subscribe to this ideal. As Alexis grappled with the effects of such a standard on women (bulimia and anorexia), her mother also questioned society's power over how we perceive ourselves, and Angela validated both writers' comments.

Another student, Viridiana, also showed a willingness to critically question her own beliefs when she wrote on a question about abandoning one's culture:

Viridiana: Am I afraid of my culture? Am I ashamed of what I am? I was born here in Georgia. Sometimes I am ashamed of Mexicans because sometimes there are some Mexicans that were born in Mexico who dress like straight up Mexicans. Maybe why I am sorta ashamed of being Mexican is because I wasn't born in Mexico and I didn't grow up with their culture. I'm not going to lie, I love being Hispanic. I love the food and I love dancing to the music. Salsa, Buchata, Merengue, and Cumbia. I love the culture but a lot of people say they're immigrants. But not all of us are. It is just the judgmental people.

Viridiana's cousin: Well, I live here in California and it is like Mexico number 2. Hahaha. Especially if you go to Tijuana because the border is right there. I guess I'm used to it because I grew up here in Cali. Where most of the Mexican population is at. Having culture is good. Not everyone is going to be the same and in life there are always going to be people who judge no matter what race or culture they are. And you shouldn't be ashamed of our roots are from. It's life.

Intrigued by Viridiana's critical questions in this entry, Angela asked the class to consider them. Angela engaged the students in a discussion around masks and why people might mask who they are, connecting to a major theme in *Bronx Masquerade* and also to pieces in their student-published newspaper and to Paul Laurence Dunbar's poem, "We Wear the Mask" (1896). We saw one such dialogue in Chapter 1.

Engaging in Critical Classroom Discussions

Jen and her students found that the power of Family Dialogue Journals to spur critical conversations and to connect them to one another emerged at unexpected times. One morning, Mack read aloud an excerpt from his journal. He and his classmates had been learning about people with different skin colors and asked their families, "When do you see people that look different than you in the world?" Mack's mother, Natalie, responded, calling for all people to work together to see beyond skin color, saying, "We all have different skin tones and can be part of the same nationality." As Mack read her words in his clear, high voice, his long, brown fingers grasping the sides of his journal, it was as if Natalie were there in the room with them. Mack finished reading and looked up at his classmates.

"Does anyone have any questions or connections?" he inquired.

Hector's hand shot into the air.

"Hector?" Mack invited.

Hector's deep chocolate-colored eyes immediately filled with tears. The mood in the room immediately became tense, as Jen, her three student teachers, and the children all realized something was wrong, *really* wrong, with Hector.

Jen frantically tried to link bits and pieces of Hector's family and home life to Mack's journal, but was unable to identify a connection between Natalie's reference to different skin tones and Hector's family.

"Someone called my house yesterday," Hector began. "He said that my family shouldn't be here because we don't speak good English, and that we should move back to Mexico. We're moving in February."

Jen's thoughts whirled with phrases like, "It's going to be okay," and "I know that must be so hard," tumbling through her brain like shoes in an empty dryer. They hit harshly against the silence in her usually chatty 1st-grade classroom. Everyone was staring at her as though they believed she would be able to say something, anything, to dissolve this tension.

Somehow, Jen spoke, determined that Hector not experience any further discomfort among his unusually quiet friends.

"Hector, your home is *here*. You have a home in Mexico, but you have a home *here*." Jen connected Hector's line of thinking to Mack's journal entry and added, "You know those people who we've talked about who thought people with different skin colors shouldn't be together?"

Michael nodded vigorously, simultaneously raising his hand and stating, "Yeah, it's just like that. Sometimes people don't like different languages, just like they didn't like different skin colors."

Michael had raised this point earlier in the year. He and his friends realized that although the students, families, and teachers that were part of their classroom community discussed valuing and respecting linguistic diversity, this was not always the case. However, they had not needed to connect these concepts in such a personal way until this moment.

Christopher said, "Hector is my best friend. I don't want him to move! I came over here because he is sad and I want to hug him. I don't want him to move!"

Christopher swiftly rose and gave Hector a long, tight hug. Jen was thankful for the simple brilliance in this action and reiterated Christopher's point. "We *all* love you very much, Hector. No matter what, you have a family in this classroom." Hector nodded bleakly, tears still on his face and looking a bit shell-shocked, as if he were reliving this event in its retelling.

Jen did the only thing she could think to do. She called for a hugging party.

Each of the students and teachers put their arms around the other, squeezing tightly and laughing, trying to convince themselves in the sheer physicality of the hugs that they were okay. In this moment, discussion around Family Dialogue Journals became a space for affirming relationships and demonstrating solidarity. It also became an opportunity to confront the reality that there were people in the world who treated others poorly because of linguistic supremacy.

This pivotal classroom event that emanated from FDJ sharing led the class to write more journal entries about the priority schools placed on speaking and writing in English. They created a project in response to the lack of books written in Spanish by coauthoring texts in multiple languages. The children engaged in impromptu discussions about how they could share their belief that all languages were equal to others, posing possibilities like sharing their books with libraries or writing newspaper articles.

Issues of prejudice entered the journals at all levels. In her high school classroom, Amber revised her curriculum to emphasize prejudice after students' responses to the prompt regarding satire in *The Importance of Being Earnest* by Oscar Wilde (1895/2003). In the play, Wilde satirized societal traditions, assumptions, and norms. Examples include rich people's views and assumptions about the "lower" classes, the intolerance for differences, the ridiculous formality used among friends, and the trivial things that were valued by the upper classes. Amber asked students to choose something in today's world that deserved satirizing. Student and parent responses included obsession with technology; sports; material objects being favored over happiness; expectations of marrying young; government spending; political campaigns; conformity; desire for money; and competition over who is better, wealthier, smarter, and so on.

Although she had planned to move away from satire, after reading the FDJ entries Amber created a writing assignment asking students to use their journal entries to compose their own satire. Amber felt that by adjusting her instruction, she was able to bring students' and parents' valuable critiques of society into the classroom so that students could discuss them; these insights were too valuable to remain on the pages of a closed journal.

Responses in the FDJs were also indicators of which issues students and parents valued, allowing Amber to utilize these themes in the curriculum to enhance student interest. She noticed that students mentioned stereotypes 27 times in their entries. The number of prompts asking about stereotypes? Zero. Clearly, this was something important to them. One student wrote about how he was followed in a store because he was a teenage African American male, profiled as a thief. His mother attributed this as normal behavior due to stereotyping. Beth wrote, "When I saw a commercial I was very offended. The insurance company is stereotyping the way teenage girls act while driving a car." As a female teenage driver, Beth was infuriated that Allstate aired a commercial that perpetuated the stereotype that girls were bad drivers and were more concerned with texting than with their safety. Amber responded, "I do not like that commercial either. They fail to mention that teenage *boys* wreck more than girls." Responding to the same prompt, Rajak, a skilled tennis player, expressed his disgust with a Metro PCS commercial that stereotyped Indians as nerds. He said, "They had strong Indian accents, said pointless things, dressed in generic telemarketing clothes, and were basically the definition of a stereotypical Indian."

To maximize on this rich FDJ discussion, Amber created an assignment centered on stereotypes so that students had a chance to dialogue with each other, not just their parents and her, about this student-valued, critical issue. Since Amber's class was reading Shakespeare's *Othello* (1604/2002), she incorporated racial stereotypes as they discussed how Othello was forced to speak for his entire race. Despite his eloquent speech, the Venetians viewed him as a "Moor" and a "barbarian" due to the color of his skin. As a supplementary text, Amber chose Derek Kirk Kim's (2004) "Hurdles," a critical cartoon text about a Korean boy's experience with prejudice. After doing a multimodal analysis, students wrote their own critical cartoon texts

COMMON CORE STANDARDS RELATED TO LITERACY, GRADE 10

CCSS.ELA-LITERACY.RL.9-10.10. By the end of grade 10, read and comprehend literature, including stories, dramas, and poems; at the high end of grades 9–10 text complexity band independently and proficiently.

CCSS.ELA-LITERACY.RI.9-10.1. Cite strong and thorough textual evidence to support analysis of what the text says explicitly as well as inferences drawn from the text.

CCSS.ELA-LITERACY.RI.9-10.2. Determine a central idea of a text and analyze its development over the course of the text, including how it emerges and is shaped and refined by specific details; provide an objective summary of the text.

CCSS.ELA-LITERACY.RI.9-10.3. Analyze how the author unfolds an analysis or series of ideas or events, including the order in which the points are made, how they are introduced and developed, and the connections that are drawn between them.

that revolved around social or racial stereotypes. This led students to a new appreciation of the pressure Othello was under, being positioned as a representative of all people of color.

If Amber had not listened to her students and analyzed their responses, she might have missed this collective concern about stereotyping. She and her students would have missed a rich and relevant opportunity to dialogue about their experiences with stereotypes and relate them to major themes in the literature.

A primary vehicle in all our classrooms for talking about issues of race, gender, social class, and other power-laden social constructs was literature. When readers in Angela's class found a single-parent household and a character in the book commenting on their life, students who also lived in single-parent homes voiced those connections. When one student shared her frustrations with being light skinned because it impacted her relationships with African American schoolmates, Angela and her students explored assumptions around skin tone in their communities. Angela added to their exploration voices from texts like Richard Rodriguez's essay "Complexion" (1983) and Christy Haubegger's essay "I'm Not Fat, I'm Latina" (1994). Examining argument texts such as these alongside the young adult novel allowed for deeper discussions and exploration of race and class. From these explorations, students then began to raise questions in the FDJs, such as the following:

1. How do we define beauty? What is considered beautiful in your culture and family? How does that compare to what society seems to say about what is beautiful?
2. Are certain jobs considered taboo in your family or culture? What are those jobs? Why are they considered off-limits?

That is not to say that these explorations and discussions happened without conflict. In all of our classrooms there have been times when student assumptions about race, gender, language, and class especially led to difficult discussions. Once in reading the excerpt from Sandra Cisneros' (1991) *The House on Mango Street*, "Those Who Don't," Angela's classroom filled with tension. A student felt that it was common sense to use caution when entering a "bad" neighborhood like the people described in the text. He gave the example of going to the football game on Friday, an away game in a community that was predominately African American and low income, and how he cautiously put his wallet in his front pocket. His assumption that the people of this community would automatically be a threat because of their race and class upset other students and Angela. The text had not challenged him to think about race and class in the critical ways Angela had hoped but had instead reaffirmed his assumptions. It was an uncomfortable discussion; Angela could have used it as a reason not to delve into such topics in the future. Instead, Angela felt that she and her students needed more opportunities to explore and discuss difficult issues in order to gain understanding of one another using multiple strategies.

For example, the first day of examining "I'm Not Fat, I'm Latina," Angela taught students, sitting in groups of three or four, to "dialogue with the text" as they read, writing on the text with their connections, questions, and highlighting quotes, words, and passages that spoke to them in some way. She asked them to stop at certain sections of the text and talk with their group about the written dialogue they had had. At each stop, students were to summarize the assigned section, share quotes and passages, raise questions, and share their connections. Once they felt they had a grasp of the material in that section, they collaboratively developed a discussion question for the section and followed the same process for the next section.

The following day Angela used the jigsaw protocol to continue the discussion of the text. First students met with their original group and gathered their thoughts from the previous day to "become experts" on their group's interpretations by examining their notes and to collaboratively decide on what was most important to share. Then they moved to new groups where they shared what their original group developed. In this new grouping Angela taught the "Save the Last Word for Me" protocol: Each student presents an idea, question, or connection they've made to the text; then others add their ideas. They work their way around the group until all have added to the first expert's idea, question, or connections. Finally, they arrive back to the original student expert and she can defend or go further with her original idea based on what has been shared. Then it is on to the next group member to present his idea. (See the National School Reform Faculty Protocols for these and other excellent discussion strategies at www.nsrfharmony.org/free-resources/protocols/a-z.)

As Angela made her way around the room, she heard students' lively debate on the author's intent at one table, while at another several students nodded as a student said her family and cultural expectations of women's bodies was much like that of Haubegger's. Latina students especially related to the challenges Christy Haubegger faced. In her Latina culture, women with full, curvaceous bodies are considered *bien cuidadas* (well cared for), but in mainstream media and the American medical profession, women like her are judged as fat. Students wondered if this prejudice solely applied to women, discussing intersections of gender and ethnicity. They made connections to film, music, and literature they had read both in school and outside of the class. It was one of those discussions that teachers dream of, but Angela reluctantly pulled them from their small groups into a whole-class discussion.

COMMON CORE STANDARDS RELATED TO CRITICAL
DISCUSSIONS OF LITERATURE

CCSS.ELA-LITERACY.RL.9-10.1: Cite strong and thorough textual
evidence to support analysis of what the text says explicitly as well as
inferences drawn from the text.

CCSS.ELA-LITERACY.RL.9-10.2: Determine a theme or central idea of a
text and analyze in detail its development over the course of the text,
including how it emerges and is shaped and refined by specific details;
provide an objective summary of the text.

CCSS.ELA-LITERACY.RL.9-10.3: Analyze how complex characters (e.g.,
those with multiple or conflicting motivations) develop over the course
of a text, interact with other characters, and advance the plot or
develop the theme.

Students shared what they had discussed in their groups. Angela wrote
their questions, connections, and ideas on the board as students shared.
From there, students discussed what to write about in the Family Dialogue
Journals that would help to show families what they had discussed and to
get an idea of where they stood on the issues with which they grappled.
Students wrote down the ideas on the board until there were eight prompts
from which to choose, reflecting both critical and personal analyses of the
social issues in Haubegger's piece. Angela described it as "one of those
magical days when everyone is so engaged in what is taking place in the
room that you lose sense of time." In the process, they addressed multiple
standards.

Responding to Resistance

While critical discussions built community and provided support for
students in several classrooms who were experiencing prejudice in their
lives, Amber encountered difficulties bringing critical inquiry into upper-middle-class homes. She struggled with student resistance, and with
how to respond to hostile entries. This was especially challenging when
the class read *As I Lay Dying* by William Faulkner and Amber introduced the issue of social class through an FDJ prompt. Amber's students expressed their belief that the majority of people have the same
opportunities as they do because they were middle class, "middle" indicating "average," and therefore the majority. While students stated that
stereotyping the poor as "lazy and ignorant" was unfair and inaccurate,
when pressed, they were not able to envision how or why people might
be living in poverty. During discussion, some students said that people

become poor because they made bad decisions in their life. Referring to the novel, Amber asked her students if this was true for each character. Students were, however, willing to reconsider their previous assumptions about why people are poor, recognizing that those born into poverty, like Faulkner's Bundrens, have less opportunities available than those of a higher economic status.

Amber's FDJ prompt invited students and families to question society's view of people affected by poverty. While Amber's students were willing to discuss the disparity between social classes and question the common depiction of the poor as being lazy and ignorant in their journals, many parents defended their lifestyle, as shown by the following entries:

- I think that poor people these days look upon the richer class as "evil" and lacking of compassion for people that have less. Some people feel that they are owed what the richer class has, but they forget or don't realize that most of these people have worked long and hard to get where they are today.
- There is, unfortunately, a part of our society who relies on others to sustain their lives. These include populations who depend on the country's social programs . . . these populations are generally a cycle that continues.
- I believe there are two kinds of poor people. Those who simply believe that money is not important, and carry on their lives in a very full way. The other kind of poor person is someone who carries out behavior that made them poor.

Amber realized that these parents had a particularly strong reaction to these prompts. She was not immune from having strong feelings herself about their entries, and her first instinct was to shoot off a message that highlighted their selfishness, indicating that they only saw the poor as leeches, bleeding them of their taxes and not as people who have dreams that are unobtainable due to their poverty. So, how does a teacher respond when students and parents write what they truly believe but it flies in the face of everything the teacher believes?

While Amber's emotional reaction to these parents was strong, the journal was created as a safe space for students and parents to share their feelings and insights about such social problems. Just because Amber did not agree with their point of view, she could not violate the safety of the journal by responding with a harsh negative judgment of their beliefs. It would not be fair to invite parents and students into this dialogue only to attack them. Therefore, Amber did not respond to the entries right away, and she composed a couple of drafts before she felt that her response did not insult the parents but still communicated her perspective.

Amber realized that the parents did not know where she was coming from. She had such a strong response because as a child, she was once dependent on the programs that the parents so vehemently criticized. However, when she thought about her biological mother, who often abused the system by trading her food stamps for drugs, she realized that the parents weren't all wrong. At the same time, if the stamps had not been available, Amber's health would have suffered. While they had a point that some individuals do abuse the system, the majority do not. Amber realized that it was the fact that they insinuated that the majority of the poor fell into this group that upset her, and realizing this, she was able to create an even-toned response that highlighted the effect of poverty on children:

> I feel that many high achievers are successful because they came from a socioeconomic status (parents) that could financially give them the resources to be successful. I feel for the parents who are unable to provide such opportunities . . . I think this plays a role in how many children born into poverty, remain in poverty.

The lesson Amber hopes to convey? Do *not* write your first gut reaction to what one might deem as a hostile entry. By taking a couple of days, Amber was able to see things from the parents' perspective and she was able to write a response that was sensitive to their anger of having their hard-earned money taken away from their children to support someone else's, while gently suggesting the necessity of such measures for the well-being of humankind.

FDJ Questions That Developed Critical Lenses

- How do you feel about the ways in which the media portrays beauty? How, if any, has this affected your body image? (Angela's classroom)
- In this week's entry, please craft a question (and response) that relates social class issues in *As I Lay Dying* to issues of class in today's world. (Amber's classroom)
- How can I use the power of my words, like Martin Luther King, Jr.? (Elyse's classroom)
- Do you think people rely on religion just so they don't have to question the unknown? (Amber's classroom)
- How can we relate social class issues in Harry Potter to those we see today? (Amber's classroom)
- What would you boycott for? (Jennifer's classroom)
- How much influence do ads have in shaping our identities? (Angela's classroom)

BRINGING FAMILIES INTO THE CLASSROOM (LITERALLY)

While we emphasize throughout this book the fact that becoming partners with families through FDJs does not require parents or caregivers to come into the classroom, sometimes they do!

As Jen noted earlier in this chapter, Family Dialogue Journals became a way for children and teachers to learn about the diverse, interesting places where everyone's families had previously lived. Geography fascinated the students, even early in their kindergarten year. They often called out, "Let's Google Earth it!" if they were unfamiliar with the location referenced in a book or lesson. It came as no surprise to Jen, then, when the children posed the question, "Where are you from?" in their FDJ. What Jen *did* find surprising, though, was the information that families shared in response to this inquiry.

During one Morning Meeting, students were sharing their family responses to the question, "*¿De dónde eres?*/Where are you from?"

"It looks like many of your families are from Michoacán, Mexico," Jen said.

Hector's hand shot into the air. "That's where my family is from, too! My family is from Michoacán!"

The children with Michoacán family connections smiled broadly at one another, as Jen pulled up Google Earth and showed the whole class where the state of Michoacán was in relation to where they all currently lived. Everyone ooohhhed and aaahhhed as they "flew" from the United States to Mexico. Children bounced up and down on the carpet, pointing and squinting as the Smart Board settled on Michoacán. Perhaps they were hoping to see the family farms their parents had described to them for years.

Jen realized what an amazing resource her students' families were in their study of geography. Writing about where they were from in the FDJs brought a study of places that might have otherwise been drab or boring to life. Their interest in the topic was heightened by their connection to one another, and Jen wanted to build upon this. So she invited a family member who wanted to share into their classroom to tell the students more about the place from which their families came. Elena, Hector's mother, agreed to come talk to the class, after Jen assured her that Mr. Oswaldo would translate from Spanish to English, that she could bring her other children, and that Jen's husband would come pick her up.

All barriers removed, Elena heartily agreed. On the morning of her visit, Hector's eyes shone brightly in anticipation of his mother walking through the door, and when she did, he ran to greet her, grabbing her hand and leading her to the chair set up at the front of the classroom, just for her. Hector proudly sat next to her.

After the children's excited chatter died down and they sat looking expectantly at her, Elena began to share. She talked about the freedom she

felt in her home country, thus weaving into the discussion a previous family dialogue journal topic on freedom; Elena recalled running through the
fields around her home, staying out all day, and knowing every one of her
neighbors.

When Mack asked her to describe what her home looked like, Elena
caught Jen's eye. She pointed to the Smart Board marker, asking if she could
draw what she remembered. "Of course!" Jen agreed. Elena drew the chickens, pigs, and horses that meandered their way in and out of the home, its
outside and inside spaces blending. This fascinated the children, most of
whom had little experience with farm animals and could only imagine dogs
or cats living in someone's home.

When the conversation concluded, the students cheered, and Elena and
Hector beamed. It was then that Elena pulled out three cakes from the bak-
ery where her husband worked, telling Jen they were a gift for her and the
students. Elena had taken time out of her day to visit, had traveled in a car
with a man she barely knew to get to the school, and yet *she* was bringing
gifts of appreciation. *What a lesson she has taught me in care and love for
others*, Jen wrote in her teaching journal later that day. *I'm sure I will learn
much more from her as the year continues.*

Jen realized how powerful it was for the children to discover their families' Michoacán connection and how important it was that she build on this
interest by extending invitations for face-to-face interactions about this topic. The success of this first visit led to others, including Jen's own father and
stepmother who told the class about their hometown in Michigan. The children asked Jen to place photographs and descriptions of each of these visits
on their classroom learning wall, where they posted their favorite learning
events from the year (Vasquez, 2004). Further, Elena's generosity taught Jen
a lesson on humility and selflessness, and she worked to weave this thread
of grace into her own life, both in and out of the classroom.

In this chapter we have shared glimpses into our classrooms and into
the coconstruction of curriculum that is connectional and critical. Through
the Family Dialogue Journal process, we are better able to (1) take into
account student interests and ideas to bring standards alive, (2) incorporate
family funds of knowledge to make curriculum relevant, (3) build on the
vast resources of cultural and linguistic diversity within and beyond our
classrooms, and (4) encourage critical thinking about social issues. In the
next chapter, we explore an equally powerful aspect of Family Dialogue
Journals: the relationships formed through this forum for dialogue.

CHAPTER 7

Creating and Deepening Relationships

Weekly communication developed relationships in both hoped for and serendipitous ways. Students and families learned more about one another, not only related to what students were learning in school, but also family history, values, and dreams. Students and teachers deepened their understanding of curriculum, shared personal and family perspectives, and formed the kinds of individual relationships that are sometimes difficult in classes of 25 to 30 students. Families and teachers, usually separate influences on students' lives, came together in the intimacy of the Family Dialogue Journal to discuss, enlighten, and support the focus of their joint care and responsibility: the students.

STUDENT–FAMILY RELATIONSHIPS

Family. Whoever that includes, family is perhaps the most powerful determinant of who we are. Families serve many roles in their children's education at home, through the journals, even in school. There were times when students needed their family to help them through a challenging situation, and the journals became a place for families to provide that support.

The last Monday in September, Malcom placed his family journal on Elyse's desk, made his lunch choice, and walked to the computer lab across the hall. Continuing to greet students in the hallway, Elyse noticed the lab teacher speaking to Malcom outside the computer lab. Malcom was looking down at the ground. The lab teacher walked him across the hall and informed Elyse that if Malcom was not going to do his work, there was no reason for him to take a spot in the lab. Malcom and Elyse walked to the front table and sat down next to each other. He told her that the work was too hard, so he did not want to do it. She told him that she had had that feeling before, too. Having thumbed through Malcom's journal earlier that morning, she knew his father's words were needed now. Elyse read aloud his father's response to Malcom's entry about fact and fiction.

Malcom a fact about you is that you are very smart. But, this year is a little challenging to you and you feel like you don't know somethings but you do. You just need to pay close attention to what it is your doing and, you will see that it is not hard as it seems. A fiction about you is you can't but you can. I love you Keep up the hard work!

Elyse finished reading and asked Malcom what he was thinking. Malcom sat a little taller in his seat, smiled, and said he was ready to go try again. She walked him across the hall and watched as he logged in and began working. Malcom needed his father's confidence in him when he was feeling inadequate, and the Family Dialogue Journal allowed that support to be present even when his father was miles away at work.

Students can also discover family history through dialogue in the FDJs, as Jennifer learned. Second grader Elizabeth gained insight to both her mom and dad's past through two separate entries.

Dear MoM
    This week we learned about what to do when you are at the book fair. When you were little did you ever visit a book fair?

Dear: Elizabeth
    I want to tell you when I went to school we didn't have a book fair, but my mom took me to the library and we borrowed books about princesses and castles. We read quickly and went more times. My mom borrowed more for me. (translated from Spanish)

Dear Family,
    This week We have been learning about cursive. We got a cursive book that has cursive letters in it. We've been wirteing our name in cursive Tell me if you ever wrote in cursive?
                                                        Love, Elizabeth

Dear Elizabeth
    Cursive writing was part of "Caligrafia" that was a signature that you Have to Pass in El Salvador to get promoted to the Next Grade.
    Yes everybody in el Salvador learn How to write that way.
                                                        loved! Dad

Because the journal entries were focused on what the students were learning, families often helped students connect school with home knowledge from various members of the family. Jayla's mom provided a poetic connection.

Dear mom
This week did work poetry iN Poetry we do Not have to Put Period IN Poetry we wrote questoNs about our Book iN a Sticky-Note. We also ShartN our questioNs with our PartNers. Have you euever writ Poetry before?

Dear Jayla,
I haven't written any poems but I do have some favorite poems that I like to read from time to time. Maya Angelou one of my favorite poets. Not only is she a poet but she also is a civil rights activist, dancer, film producer, television producer, playwright, film director, author, actress, professor. Wow, Ms. Angelo is very talented. Set goals and you can achieve them.
P.S. My favorite poem by Maya Angelou is "Phenomenal Woman"

As you can imagine, this led the class to explore the poetry of Maya Angelou, Jayla's mom's favorite poet!
Several of our students at all grade levels dialogued with siblings either occasionally or regularly. In Jennifer's 2nd grade, Maria's "oldest" sister provided a little lecture about a civil rights giant after Maria wrote in her journal,

Dear Sister,
This week we learned about martin Luther King. Tell me what you learned about Martin Luther King. Love Maria

Dear Maria,
I am very happy that you are learning about a great man like martin Luther King, Jr. I learned that thanks to him we can go to school with a variety of different kids from different race. We can interact with different kinds of people and that the color of people's skin doesn't matter. We are all equal and we deserve to be treated equal. Every person in this world is like a brother and a sister to each other. Last but not least he gave a very famous speech named, "I have a dream . . ." Martin Luther King Jr. was assassinated. His children and wife were left alone without a dad and a father. I hope you learn something from this.

Sincerely and with Love,
Your oldest sister

One of Jennifer's students wrote to an older brother as they were learning cursive.

Dear family,
    This week we have been learning about cursive. We got a cursive book that has cursive letters in it. We've been prackticing writing our name in cursive. Tell me about a time you rote in printe.

Love, Alejandro

Dear Alejandro
    I never learn how to write in cursive and I don't know how to write in cursive but you can show me how to write in cursive when you learn. Keep up to good work.

Joycelyne's older brother also wrote in her journal that week.

DeAr fAMily,
    This week we hAve been learning About cursive. We got A cursive book that hAs cursive letters in it. We've been prAticing writing our nAme in cursive. Do you Mostly write in cursive or in print?

Love Jocelyne

Dear Jocelyne
    I always write in print and I'm super exited for you to bring the note book so I could write in cursive.

Student–family relationships deepened through FDJs in Jennifer's class when the families showed their support of academic content and its application to everyday living, as well as providing encouragement to the student. Here Jayla's mom shows support for the journals themselves. Jayla wrote,

Thiss week we have Been LearniNiNg aBout PumPKiNS. We made a pumPkin seeds and did a pumpkiN activity. WheN you Were Littls did you do aNy of Those?

Jayla P.S MoM I Love

Hello, Jayla
    I'm super excited for you! I just love the thought of reading your journal each weekend. To answer your question yes we carved pumpkins and make pumpkin pies. Today we plan to carve pumpkins and make halloween cupcakes.

Love, Mom

There were often indications that conversations that began in the classroom continued at home. Jazmin asked her father the following:

Dear DaD,
    We have been learning about Black History Month. We learned
that Rosa parks' refusal to give up her seat on the bus helped start a
boycott. What would you boycott for?

Sincerly Jazmin

Dear Jazmin
    Good question. I don't know what I would Boycott. Maybe we
can sit down and talk about this over the weekend.

Sincerely, Dad

More often than not, families and students expressed similar perspectives about a topic. The students wrote their perspectives and the parents
usually built on what the child said. However, there were times when a family member challenged what a student wrote. For one family in Angela's 9th
grade, this created a dynamic dialogue between father and son.
    The class was studying values and beliefs. They read various excerpts
from the textbook, such as the story of Sibi from the Mahabharata, the story
of Ruth from the Bible, the Fisherman and the Jinnee from *1,001 Nights*,
parts of the Rig Veda and the Qu'ran, and a few Zen parables. Angela used
the television series *30 Days,* produced by Morgan Spurlock (Landgraf, Silverman, Owens, Spurlock, & Cutler, 2005), to have students consider the
challenges of taking on someone else's point of view and living a new lifestyle. Specifically, she showed them "Muslims in America," which focuses on
a Christian man, Dave, living with a Muslim family for a month. As part of
the show's premise, Dave has to abide by the family's household expectations
and immerse himself in the Muslim culture. He is expected to eat the way the
Muslim family eats, worship the way they worship, and try to understand as
much as he can about the Arabic language and Islamic religion. The show also
illustrated the discrimination and stereotyping Muslims in America face daily.
    After watching and discussing the program and reading the various
texts in the unit, the students and Angela developed prompts for the Family
Dialogue Journals. One was, Would you be able to live with someone different for 30 days or do something different for 30 days? Why or why not?
A second question focused on stereotypes. With each swap, Angela always
reminded students that it was not enough to just write and answer the question, but that they needed to provide the context from which the question
was developed so that families would understand what was taking place
in class. Students could also tailor the question as needed in order to get a
response from their family members. They were always welcome to use one
of their own questions instead of the class-generated topics.
    Radin chose to write about the show for the second swap because it
raised a very specific question for Radin. Where the class-generated question

about stereotypes was more about personally being stereotyped, Radin wanted to know if his father had ever stereotyped others. It was here that Angela became very interested in the father–son dynamic. Radin wrote:

> Last week we watched a show called 30 Days. In this show a man had to live 30 days with a Muslim family. This man was a devout Catholic and had to follow all of their traditions and costoms. Like many Americans, this man's image of Muslims was that they were all anti-American terrorists. However, after spending a month in this Muslim community, he relized that Muslims are peaceful people who believe in many Christian teachings. He also learned that you can't stereotype a whole group based on the actions of a few. Were you ever in a situation where you stereotyped a whole because of a few?

Radin's father responded:

> Stereotyped a group because of the actions of a few? Excellent question. Currently I serve in the Georgia Army National Guard, as a member of the military I believe that we are stereotyped daily. Both with positive and negative stereotypes. Everyone has an opinion about the Army and over the course of history the opinions have varied from praise and thankfulness to hatred and disgust. As with the movie you watched, you cannot judge someone by the actions of others that maybe in the same culture, group, affiliation, or beliefs. You have to look at a person's actions and how they live their life in order to form your opinion of them. My grandfather told me that you are not only judged by your own actions but by those you associate with as well. I have to agree and disagree with that statement. I agree because if you put yourself in a position that causes doubt in your character, then you are to blame as well. I disagree because just because you associate with someone you can't control their actions. A little away from your question, but the point I want to make is that as a person we can not judge anyone but ourselves and live our life to make the most positive it can be for us and those we care about.

Angela continued the dialogue:

> I really couldn't agree more with each of the perspectives you all take here. I think living your life in a way that illustrates your characters to others and being the best person you can be for those around you certainly are important. I've often been judged for being from the South—some good and some bad. The thing that most upsets me is when people assume that I think or see things the same way they do

simply because we are from the same place—the South. I've also faced those that see the South as backwards and all based on farming. Those are the people I shrug off and get a good laugh at because they see the South so narrowly.

During the third prompt, the class explored what it meant to take a critical stance and continued to think about values and beliefs. Angela used several essays from National Public Radio's series *This I Believe*, as well as music and advertisements. Students generated topics based on various ways of taking a critical stance. They could write about a specific belief they held and why. They could write about an essay from the *This I Believe* collection and why they agreed with the stance the author took. They were asked to bring in a song they felt took a critical stance and share it with the class. In the Family Dialogue Journal, they could share the song with their parents, explain the message they took from the song, and ask their parents to share a song with them. The last topic focused on media's influence. Radin wrote on the last option: How much influence do ads have in shaping our identities?

> Last week we took a look at ads and how they influence our lives and "dictate our society." In my opinion, ads do not dictate my life. I do buy "brand" products, but I don't base who I am around them. Ads don't control people's lives. People just obsess over the "brand" name. How do you feel ads and brands influence our society?

Radin's father responded as follows:

> Unfortunately, I have to disagree with Radin. Ads are designed to influence, if not companies would not spend so much money getting the word out about a product. Think about it like this . . . all of the toy commercials around Christmas time influence children, who influence their parents, who in turn buy the "next hot toy" to make their child feel special. Or maybe the Automotive industry, buy Mercedes or BMW, buy AMERICAN (Ford or Chevy), become eco-friendly and go green . . . I feel that in order to not be influenced by ads or brands you have to do your research. You cannot be an impulse shopper just because the TV or radio says this is what you need. Today too many Americans are not smart shoppers, as with the Europeans. The hot ticket item makes you feel a part of a group or like you fit in, so therefore you buy. I believe in the old saying, "you get what you pay for." Does the brand do everything the ad says it will do, if so then it's worth the investment. If not, then you learned something from the purchase and hopefully won't make the same mistake in the future.

Ads do influence use every day. Our knowledge will either increase the ads or make us look at other options. In the end it's your money and your time spent on believing or dismissing the ad.

Much like Radin's father, many parents used the journal to impart wisdom to their children. It is through these exchanges that Angela learned about what a family valued most. One exchange that best illustrates this was between Valerie and her mother, Gladys. Valerie wrote about masks and masking for the fourth swap:

Everyone wears masks. People wear one every day and however they please. Some wear fake masks and others wear one to hide their identities in order to fit in. I don't wear a mask, when it comes to showing [my] ability and passion to do stuff. But when it comes to friends, out of all my friends, I only trust 2 of them. One including Camilla. I don't need a mask to be around them. I get annoyed so when someone pisses me off, I give them that fake mask. Teehee. What masks have you worn in the past? How often do you where them?

Valerie's mother replied:

Vava, Within friends life is cherished and the good and bad times are passed. To know what it means to be a friend, all you need to do is be one. It can't be said that friendship is not real if we are not really trustworthy, without masks, and value what the other person means to us without differences (color, sex, social classes). In friendship, each one of our lives responds differently, but at the same time, we come together, like the sun and the rain; when the rays of the sun come through, the rain stops.

With love,
Gladys

Angela added:

Masks are tough because we don't want to wear them and then we find we do. It protects us when we are around those we don't know or don't trust. I try not to wear a mask around you all. I feel like if I want you to be honest with me, I need to be honest with you. So masking wouldn't allow that to happen.

Angela sent home a survey at the end of the study to gain feedback from both students and families. Camilla's mother wrote, "The thing that I enjoyed most was learning about Camilla's point of view on all of the topics discussed, and I thank you for that, because they turned into long conversations between us."

In Amber's AP English class, parents often took turns writing in the journals: Mom one week, Dad the next. She loved that dads, granddads, and stepdads were participating because in some homes, the education of children is considered "women's work." In Beth's journal, her older brother, who was 22 and in college, responded to the entries. In this way, Beth was able to get his perspective on many of the topics and how they related to college life.

In one entry about commercials, Kelly's mom wrote about the "Cialis" commercial and how uncomfortable it made her, especially when her children were there. Amber thought it was brave that this woman addressed the topic of adult sex with her daughter. She could have chosen a commercial that was less uncomfortable, but she used the FDJ as a venue to address it, possibly because it was more comfortable to write about it than talk about it. In this way, the journal provided an outlet for the mother to express to her daughter her discomfort when watching this commercial with her daughter in the room, allowing them to better understand each other.

Week after week, parents interacted with, learned from, counseled, and advised their children from kindergarten through 12th grade. Relationships may have developed new dimensions through this written forum because (1) students and teachers asked questions in the FDJs that families might not have discussed previously; (2) families had the luxury (or pressure, whichever it might have felt like during any given week) of time to sit down, talk, and write about a topic; and (3) FDJs were generally free of the baggage of specific behavior issues since they were focused on academic content.

FDJ QUESTIONS THAT DEEPENED FAMILY RELATIONSHIPS

- What are your hopes and dreams for me this year? (Jen's classroom)
- Where do you share family stories? (Jen's classroom)
- At what times have you lost hope? Why? (Angela's classroom)
- How was your name chosen? (Angela's classroom)
- What was school like for you, and did you ever think about dropping out? (Joseph's classroom)
- What do you want my class to know about our family? (Jennifer's classroom)
- Where are you from? (Jen's classroom)
- What is the biggest struggle you've faced? How did you deal with/ handle it? In what ways did it change you or affect you? (Angela's classroom)

STUDENT–TEACHER RELATIONSHIPS

Family Dialogue Journals can be a space where students think about how they present themselves and how they want others to view them. They can even challenge images that teachers may have about them. An exchange with Sierra allowed Angela to learn something she did not know about Sierra and for Sierra to see Angela in a different way as well. During the reading of *They Poured Fire on Us from the Sky* (Deng, Deng, Ajak, & Bernstein, 2005), Sierra's question was, "What is the biggest struggle you've faced? How did you deal/handle it? In what ways did it change you or affect you?" Sierra responded:

> The biggest struggle I faced was in my freshman year of high school. I got paneled [sent to the alternative school]. I thought it was the worst time of my life. I thought I would never see any of my friends and I thought, since the school would be horrible. Since I had no choice, I just counted down the days til I had left of being out of that school. My first day was horrible, but then as I got to know people it became all right. As I adjusted to the school, I became to like it because the classes were smaller and I learn better in small classes. The final last day of school, I was happy to get out of there but I didn't at the same time because of the people and teachers I met. Even though I got paneled, I think everything happens for a reason.

It was surprising for Angela to read this entry from Sierra. Angela had no idea that Sierra had been in the alternative school the year before. Angela does not look at discipline records of students unless she feels it will help her in understanding the student better; she never looks at them prior to meeting the student and working with them for several weeks. Sierra never gave Angela a reason to look into her disciplinary past; she had a good sense of humor and smiled often. Typically reserved during whole-class discussions, Sierra would work with peers in small groups. There are students who consider attending the alternative school to be a sort of badge of honor and who are quick to let others know that they spent time there, but Sierra did not. Knowing how reserved Sierra had been through the year and that sharing something like this may have been challenging for her, Angela wanted to honor her response. She wrote in the journal:

> When you go through a test like that, you learn what you are capable of handling. I was suspended from UGA because I turned in the same paper—my paper—twice to two different professors. The issue was that I didn't ask permission and because I didn't change enough of the original paper before turning it in to the second professor. I got in trouble, took an F on the paper and had to take additional hours to

make up for the course since I needed the hours to graduate. It also caused me to postpone graduation by a year because I was suspended for a semester. Dealing with it was really difficult and horrible, but it made me stronger and I realized how I would handle a situation when my character might be questioned which was a really important thing to learn.

Since Sierra showed Angela a part of her past that she might not have shared otherwise, Angela felt that she needed to do the same. It was risky for Angela to share, but it perhaps showed Sierra that one aspect of her past did not have to shape the rest of her future. Opening up helped Angela to build relationships in ways that may not have been built without the Family Dialogue Journals.

During the journal exchange that focused on education, Jessica wrote about her dreams and goals, and her mother responded. Through this exchange, Angela learned so much about how Jessica saw herself as a student and an agent for change within her own life. Jessica shared the following:

My dream/goal in life is to make it in the world. By being successful and doing something I love and getting money. I want to be an owner to something I enjoy. To me that will be a long way but to me my start to my dream/goal is finishing high school and of course college. My dream needs a college education because I need to know how to reach a point in my live to be successful. I need education to reach what I want. Without college it would be more difficult to get to being the owner/manager of my dream. By getting an education I will prove my skills and take on life and I will make it in life. With me having an education and a dream, I could probably do anything. College to me is very important. I need it for my goal in life. What was your dream, when you were my age and did it require college? If so is it important?

Jessica's mother, Maria, responded:

My dream/goal was to come to the United States of America. Why? Because I wanted a better life than the one I had back home in Guatemala. This goal, I didn't really need a college education. I just wanted a good life and start out fresh with my life. My Aunts didn't really push me to head to college. They wanted me to have a better life and that was my dream.

During her culture project presentation to the class, Jessica shared that graduating from high school and going to college was an important dream for her because she would be the first in her family to do so. Learning about students' goals, and how those goals grew out of their unique family experiences and expectations, helped Angela to build stronger relationships with them—a primary goal in her teaching.

Another aspect of our relationships with students was that students often felt they could come to us with concerns about family issues because we had knowledge of students' families through the journals. As teenagers, Amber's students were very attuned to the dynamics of the family, and often expressed their troubles to her. When their relationship with one parent or both was strained, students seemed to feel that the dialogue with Amber was sacred and continued that communication even if there was a breakdown in family communication. The FDJ process helped Amber develop this trust, for if dialoguing about home had not been attempted, students may not have felt comfortable coming to Amber with their problems, missing out on a supportive ally.

Student–teacher relationships are also fostered through the journals because they give students a venue in which they can express their feelings about the teacher, to the teacher. When responding to a prompt that asked students if they viewed sarcasm as hurtful or humorous, one of Amber's students stated that he thought sarcasm was funny in comedy television programs and in stories but that it hurt his feeling when it was directed at him. Paul said that lots of times when he asked a friend or a teacher a question, they answered him sarcastically. To her horror, Amber realized that she had responded to one of Paul's questions sarcastically just that week, trying to be funny. When Amber answered questions sarcastically, she thought it helped students to figure out the answer for themselves instead of asking her all the time, trying to break their dependence on her as having the answer to everything. While she was joking, Amber realized that it made students feel insecure and unintelligent—something she would *never* do intentionally. She began to monitor her responses, being careful to avoid sarcasm.

This particular question in the FDJ gave Paul an opportunity to tell Amber how he felt in an "academic" arena, so it did not seem awkward or forced. It also gave Amber the opportunity to tell him how she knew she has been guilty of sarcasm with her students and that it was very helpful to her that he told her how it made him feel. In this case, the FDJ served as a venue in which to communicate feelings about interactions between student and the instructor. It enhanced the student–teacher relationship by providing a means to express feelings and make amends without having to address the teacher face to face, an action that many students would never attempt.

FAMILY–TEACHER RELATIONSHIPS

Family Dialogue Journals opened regular dialogue that might not otherwise occur between home and school, in part because we left behavior and academic struggles for other types of communication (phone calls, conferences, emails). The FDJs often provided new perspectives on topics, and allowed families and teachers to get to know one another in ways that are impossible during many school events (e.g., Science Night, Field Day, Open House) where many families are present.

Upon receiving her class roster, Elyse was warned about a student in her class and the minimal help she would receive from home. Elyse's first attempts to contact home went unanswered. Then they began journaling. Each week Santrese was one of the first students to bring her journal back. The entries expressed love and encouragement toward her daughter. Santrese's mother shed light on some of the struggles she endured as a single mother who worked long hours. The journal provided a positive line of communication that was flexible enough to fit into her schedule.

When Elyse's 2nd-graders wrote about their New Year's resolutions, a mother wrote that she was trying to run more, which was Elyse's goal, too. The parent and teacher periodically used the journals to check in with each other's progress, celebrate an achievement, or share a challenge.

Stephanie always tried to be supportive of her 3rd-grade students both inside and outside of class. When they had a soccer game, she'd go. If they invited her to a birthday party, she was there. But those sweet experiences depended on invitations from the children. When she implemented FDJs, more families reached out to her and invited her to special family, church, and community events.

Camellia was a student who often invited Stephanie to family events. Stephanie attended her birthday party in the fall and later, her parents' wedding at their church. Another invite came as their class studied segregation. This led them to some children's literature about Harriet Tubman, a former slave who led her people to freedom by way of the Underground Railroad. Around this same time, Camellia's church was hosting a play about Harriet Tubman's journey. She and her mother invited Stephanie to attend the play with them on a Friday evening. Even though Camellia was not a part of the play and neither was her mother, it was important for her to embrace important learning outside the classroom. Camellia and Stephanie referred back to the play many times during their class discussions and Morning Meeting chats.

Another student, a dancer both at school and in her community, invited Stephanie to watch her local dance group perform at a theater downtown. She was such a proud teacher as she cheered her on. Attending Shawntina's performance allowed Stephanie the opportunity to speak with her mom and older brother, who were also in the audience. She asked her students every day to participate in her passion of learning, and it was always enjoyable when she was able to participate in their passions, as well.

Stephanie knows some people may pose the question, "How did the journals create these experiences? I'm invited to sporting events and birthday parties all the time and I don't use Family Dialogue Journals." She would say that they are right. She had invitations to things before she began using these journals. But if teachers want to create strong relationships with children and families, Family Dialogue Journals help initiate and later solidify those relationships. Stephanie wasn't sure if the journals opened up the lines of communication so that she felt more included in family events or if the experiences outside of school helped the parents and students feel more willing to write in the journals, but she knew that both scenarios contributed to overall parent–teacher–child relationships.

Amber also developed personal relationships with members of her students' families. For example, Mehal's mother was particularly forthcoming about her experiences growing up as a daughter of Indian parents and expressed how she would have loved to have been a teacher, but her parents wanted her to become a doctor. This desire to be a teacher linked Mehal's mother and Amber, for they both wanted to educate children. In addition, Mehal told her mother that Amber was in graduate school pursuing her doctorate. A doctor herself and very in tune with the lifestyle of a working student, Mehal's mother sent Amber a comic strip that communicated her understanding of Amber's busy and hectic schedule. When Mehal graduated that May, her mother wished Amber the best of luck in her studies. While this event seems small, it shows how the FDJs allowed parents and teachers to become invested in one another's' personal dreams and endeavors, genuinely caring about one another's' future and happiness.

In Amber's second year of including FDJs in her classroom, one parent referred to a near-death experience. Interested, Amber asked the parent if she was comfortable elaborating on the experience so that she could better understand her perspective on the student-generated prompt (which happened to be provided by her child): "Do you think that people rely on religion so they don't have to question the unknown?" The question stemmed from a class discussion of *As I Lay Dying* by William Faulkner about the nature of knowledge and questioning our own presumed knowledge, which is an essential element of critical literacy. The question was risky since it was about religion, and Amber expected strong responses based on individual views.

This parent wrote that she was injured and saw a light that she chose not to go toward, choosing life over death. Based on this experience, she believed that God should not be questioned. Amber asked the parent if her conviction in God and lack of questioning was based on her near-death experience—because she experienced it, she didn't have any questions—and if that made her unique from the majority of the population, who had no experience with the afterlife. The parent gave Amber the full account of her experience, agreeing that it was unique. At the end of her narrative, she thanked Amber for asking her to share, stating that no one had ever asked her to write about it before and that she enjoyed it. Amber viewed this exchange as an example of how continued dialogue played a role in validating a parent's experience and its relation to the class discussion. Also, by encouraging the parent to share her life experience through a written narrative, it further engaged the parent in the writing process and, therefore, Amber's academic classroom practices, while also showing the parent's child that various forms of writing are valued in their household.

EXPANDING THE CIRCLE OF RELATIONSHIPS

In addition to the relationships we've explored in this chapter, we were delighted to discover that Family Dialogue Journals extended our classroom communities in unanticipated ways. Families learned about and from other families, students got to know peers and their families, and families knew much more about the learning, experiences, and questions of their children's classmates. We close with one such circle of friendship.

One day during Morning Meeting in Jen's 1st grade, a few students shared aloud their responses to the question, "Where do you see people who have a different skin color?" Because the students' own racial backgrounds were so diverse, and because they often read books about children and families who have different skin colors, this topic had interested them for a long time. So they decided to ask their families about it. The families' responses generated much conversation, as each child reading his or her journal called on two friends to ask questions or make connections to what they read.

After a friend shared her mother's belief that all people should get along regardless of skin color, Lorena said, "I have a connection to your mom, because yesterday when we shared my home journal, my mom said the same thing about getting along with all people." Lorena was not only connecting her journal to a fellow student's; she was connecting *her mother's* perspective to *her friend's mother's* perspective. The journal was a powerful tool for helping the children bring in their families' voices, and for recognizing the commonalities between these voices. Though these two families were from different cultural backgrounds, one African American and one Guatemalan, Lorena pointed out that they held similar values regarding the fair treatment of people. In this moment, Lorena brought the women together, illustrating shared beliefs while discussing a topic many adults find uncomfortable.

Jen realized that by sharing students' Family Dialogue Journals, she and the children were creating a space where relationships expanded and flourished. These relationships defied spatial boundaries, as Lorena connected two women who were present not in physical form but in written voice. When Lorena acknowledged these similarities, she strengthened relationships that existed both within and beyond the classroom walls.

Jen's commitment to Family Dialogue Journals grew as she recognized that they fostered relationships beyond the three voices in each journal. Connecting families with one another in an increasingly isolated world was just one of the many reasons teachers, students, and families valued the three-way journal process, as we'll see in the next chapter.

CHAPTER 8

Learning from Students and Families

At the conclusion of their second year together, Jen and her students faced the task of brainstorming and writing their final Family Dialogue Journal entries. Jen thought that, considering end-of-the-year fatigue and the children's desire for summer vacation, she might hear a group "yes!" upon announcing that this was their last entry.

But instead of relief, the air went still when she made the announcement.

"Aaawww," Mack breathed in a low, quiet voice. Others simply stared at her.

Jen and the students decided to write to their families about their favorite learning opportunities in both kindergarten and 1st grade, a topic that brought into focus just how much time they had spent together. To their families, they posed the question, "What do you remember us learning about over the past two years?"

The children brainstormed an extensive list of memorable activities, each eliciting laughter and excitement. Jen reflected that, without this final journal activity, these activities might have remained buried under newer memories. Yet here they were, recalling the "dirt pudding" students made to show layers of soil in kindergarten, giggling about how Google Earth had helped them to discover that the Gingerbread Baby lived in Hawaii (it's true—look it up!), and making vegetable soup to learn the parts of a plant. Everyone smiled as they thought about planting a peach tree like Mama Miti, one of their favorite world changers, and writing multilingual books to ensure they represented their friends' home languages in the library.

Jen's students wrote in their journals that day, to carry them home and set them on a kitchen counter or coffee table one last time. For the first time in many weeks, every child brought back their Family Dialogue Journal within a few days, and every child shared what they and their families enjoyed most about their 2 years together.

Through their obvious disappointment that this was their last journal entry, and their participation in bringing each journal back to share one more time, Jen's students showed their long-term enthusiasm for this home–school partnership activity. The process the children used to create their entries, the length of their entries, and the way they shared with their friends and family had changed immensely over their 2 years together. Yet the twofold goal at the heart of the activity remained the same: to blur the lines between home and school by sharing these two worlds and to deepen relationships and learning among families, children, and teachers.

A few things are probably clear by now: most of us found the Family Dialogue Journal process highly beneficial in forming partnerships with families that supported student learning, for bridging home and school knowledge and perspectives, and for initiating and sustaining relationships. The process has not always been smooth and not equally effective in all circumstances. We are constantly revising, reinventing, and reflecting on how the FDJ process can best meet the needs of all involved. To that end, we sought the opinions and advice of families and students, as well as one another.

FAMILY PERSPECTIVES ON FDJS

Families are essential to the success of Family Dialogue Journals, and we valued their perspectives about the process. We asked families about their journaling experiences, sent home surveys, made phone calls, and reflected on the journaling process with families throughout the year(s), not just at the end. We learned processes that worked better for families, and we learned what they valued about FDJs and the opportunity to be active participants in their child's schooling.

Flexibility

FDJs allow for flexible use. The procedures can be adapted to fit individual classroom needs. For example, one classroom may send the journals home every Friday while another might do so every other Tuesday. Likewise, the communication is flexible, as it allows families to respond when and how they are able. Some families may have the same person respond while others may change responders or have multiple family members respond to a single entry.

This flexibility is one reason that Lorena's and Hector's mothers, Rosalita and Elena, identified the FDJs as their favorite form of communication when Jen asked. Elena said, "The best way to talk is to send home the journal." Similarly, Rosalita commented that she preferred the journal to the phone, because "if somebody asks me about something, maybe it's difficult for me to understand." Rosalita's comments show how additional time to read and respond can be helpful to speakers of English as a second language. Further, FDJs invite families to participate in school learning activities without requiring costly or timely resources, such as transportation or child care.

Still, despite the flexibility and time allotted to respond, some families struggle to find time to read their child's entries. One parent reflected that the journal forced her to sit and read her son's writing despite her busy schedule. She wrote, "I would not have read his responses if I hadn't had to respond myself."

Student Growth

Parents (as well as teachers and the students themselves) were able to see their child's progress in writing and/or content knowledge throughout the year. Elyse's 2nd-grade and kindergarten parents commented on the power of seeing their children's growing abilities to express their ideas and opinions. In Jen's classroom, Mack's mother, Natalie, flipped back through Mack's kindergarten and 1st-grade journals. She was floored by the growth, in both illustrations and written words. It was "better and better each time that he wrote," she reminisced. "I was very impressed with that. And I was able to communicate with him and he understood me, and it's amazing!" Mack's father, Patrick, agreed. He told Jen how much of a family activity the FDJs had become in their home. As he talked about how interesting it was to learn that children Mack's age often used "sound" spelling in their writing, he said, "Natalie knew what he wrote, whether it was spelled correctly or not, and she showed me how to actually read it." FDJs functioned as a way to track Mack's progress in literacy, and as an opportunity to come together as a family.

The journals also illustrated other forms of growth, such as individual thought and exploration of ideas. When Angela asked families to consider what the process meant for them, Alexis's mother responded:

> To be part of the class in a way, to see how Alexis thinks in situations, to participate on this level, to go back and forth on ideas was amazing to me. Overall, I gained insight to Alexis' thoughts. I saw her in a different light; not just being my daughter, but being her own person.

Participation in Learning

"What did you learn at school today?"

"Nothing."

With FDJs, this classic response is much less likely. As one parent in Stephanie's classroom put it, "Family weekend journals are a fun and creative way to pass the activities you've done at school on to your parents at home. Throughout the year I've learned a lot about what you've learned and I've truly enjoyed reading it." A parent in Angela's class stated, "It kept me aware of classwork and just knowing of what was being done and discussed in the class. Alexis and I had an open dialogue about the class."

In addition to the content, a parent in Elyse's classroom felt that the writing format was beneficial. She wrote to her daughter, "I absolutely enjoyed reading your journal writings this year. I think the journal offered a chance for you to practice on your handwriting and writing your thoughts on paper in a semiformal manner. For me I think it was a very interesting way for us to share with one another." Jennifer's families valued learning about classroom processes. Several reported asking their children about what they had shared from the FDJ. One student reported, "My aunt and mom always said what did your class think about my letter."

The journals also allow families to provide meaningful input and feel personally connected to the classroom experience. Maria's mom, a parent in Jennifer's classroom, liked it because "it made me feel helpful to you. I also think that our journal helped us learn about our family history." Elizabeth's mom, another parent in Jennifer's classroom, was happy because "the journal makes me feel more involved in your education. I am very happy to be part of your class and share with you the experiences at school" (translated from Spanish). Others felt being able to share their knowledge and experiences was beneficial. For example, one family member from Stephanie's classroom said, "I do enjoy the family weekend journal because I get to sit and read all the new and fun things you learned and share with you some of the things that I have learned." Similarly, a parent in Angela's classroom said, "The process has meant more involvement with my son's schoolwork and the ability to review and participate with him. I've learned about things my son has on his mind even though he may not vocalize them."

Several families valued the academic conversations with their children. In Jen's room, Alejandro's sister said, "This has even taught me things I didn't even know about. It makes me really happy to still learn new things." A family member in Stephanie's classroom agreed: "Yes! We do enjoy the weekend journal because tell us about you. What you are learning, we learning, too. For us is like a newspaper."

Parents in Amber's classes said that FDJs created a link to their teenager's thoughts. Kelly's mom stated, "It let me see my child as a student and I see how and why she feels about different topics. You should keep this project next year so that parents can actually see how their 'teenagers' are thinking about things." Similarly, Mehal's mother said she enjoyed learning about her daughter's "perspective on certain subjects." Parents felt their teenagers distancing themselves in order to discover their individuality; the journals provided valuable insight into who their children were becoming.

Open Communication

Many families felt the journals were a beneficial form of communication. Jazmin's dad, whose child was in Jennifer's class, said, "Our family journal was great. I had a good time doing this all year long. This journal helped us learn, communicate, and share things. Even tho the school year is over, I think we should do this to keep communication."

The FDJs also spurred family discussion that may not have occurred otherwise. Amber's families reported that the dialogue started in the journal was often continued through family discussion. Beth's mother wrote, "I feel that the family dialogue journal has created great discussions amongst our family and Mrs. Simmons." Mehal's mother wrote that "the journal it was one big conversation and it made me comfortable," mirroring Beth's mother's positive experience with having a teacher who was involved in their family discussions.

Some families looked at the FDJ as an opportunity to see if their children had taken heed of the lessons they had imparted. Radin's father shared:

> It was a great opportunity for our family to see the core values we try to establish with our children are getting through to them. The knowledge and understanding that my son has are independent thoughts and he doesn't have to feel as though he has to follow the popular thought process. Radin has stronger opinions than most kids his age, and given the opportunity to share them, you will be surprised at his intelligence.

Critical Feedback

For most families, Family Dialogue Journals are an unfamiliar way of participating in schools. Some families found them less meaningful than the majority, and it was important for us to listen to their perspectives, too. We never forced families to respond nor made students feel inadequate if they didn't write. Some parents did not understand the purpose of the three-way conversation. A parent of one of Amber's students said that she didn't understand the point; her responses reflected this feeling. Her child wrote that she was disappointed that her family was not more engaged in responding to her writing.

Some parents saw the FDJs as too time-consuming. Maggie, a mother of one of Jen's students, had mixed feelings about FDJs. When Jen asked her whether she believed they were an effective learning tool, she said, "The journals were a good idea, because it let the kids write about what they've experienced and then they come and ask their parents." She loved the fact that Michael was excited to discuss each entry, and she said, laughing, that "even before I would go in the journal we would talk about it." However, she noted that with her schedule as a teacher, she was not able to do as much with the journal as she would have liked. Instead, she would have preferred a variety of communication options over the 2 years, suggesting "something small" like a graphic organizer she could have completed with Michael. "Some parents probably loved it," Maggie concluded, but it was not the most conducive tool for her.

STUDENT PERSPECTIVES ON FDJS

It is the students' enthusiasm for the FDJ process that ultimately fuels and bridges the conversation from school to home and back. To build and maintain excitement and urgency, we reflected with students on the purpose of the FDJs throughout the year(s). We invited students to share their thinking through their journals and about their journals, encouraging them to learn individual differences among themselves and their families, practice problem solving, and challenge their thinking. Our students expressed the value of the journals as catalysts to conversations, as venues for learning from others, and as a necessary push to express their own ideas through writing.

Communicating with Families

Students repeatedly reported that the FDJs opened a door for extended and meaningful conversations between themselves and their families. Angela's student, Jimmy, shared that the FDJs were "conversation starters with my parents, my mom specifically," and that he gained "a better understanding of how my parents feel about things. I noticed that it's easier to talk to my parents about anything I need to talk about." A peer noted that the journals helped him to connect with his mother, brother, and sister through topics that they might not usually discuss at home.

The journals sparked new conversations in homes and gave students new perspectives on their family members. Amber's student, Mehal, stated, "I learned a lot about my mom. Maybe it was because I never asked her, but this journal was eye-opening. I never knew she would have similar perspectives as me. After all, she always portrays herself to be from a foreign planet." Likewise, Rajak revealed, "I learned a lot more about my family than I did about myself, but I valued it greatly." Alejandro, Jen's student, explained, "I feel great because I get to know more about my family . . . we ask questions that aren't yes or no and we get a conversation."

The journals sparked academic conversations in students' personal lives. The personal relevance made the content meaningful and memorable. Jennifer's student Saffiyyah pointed out, "It feel's Great because ti's you family that your learing about." The journals helped some students learn about family traditions, history, opinions, and interests. Elizabeth wrote, "I didn't know that dad been on t.v and that my mom liked Fariy tales. . . . I Loved wirting in it seing to know how parents feel about it." While students learned about their parents' personal experiences and beliefs, they also realized, like Beth stated, that her "parents care about my school work and genuinely want to know what I'm learning about." Angela's student, Alexis, gained confidence in her relationship with her mother, sharing, "I have noticed that I'm really not scared anymore to tell my mom how I feel about different things."

Connecting School and Home

Some students expressed strong positive feelings at seeing their parents and teacher interact regularly. Missy wrote,

> It is also interesting and unique to see interaction between my dad and Mrs. Simmons [Amber]. Usually, there is one day in the school year in which parents communicate, so [for] such interaction to occur regularly has been exciting . . . Through the journal, I have seen my teacher and dad's opinion on topics we may not regularly discuss at home.

Several students expressed how much they valued having a teacher take an interest in their personal and cultural lives. Chad wrote, "I've come to realize that me and Mrs. Dean have more things in common than I had thought before." As difficult and as awkward as the process may have been at the beginning for some of the students, many seemed to value learning about Angela, who had been willing to share openly and personally. As the FDJ process progressed, she found that the reward was a true community of learners. Discussions and readings of texts were coconstructed, and students valued hearing from one another, as well as Angela. One student shared, "It has shown me that there are teachers who do actually care to connect, or at least know more about their students. It's rare, in my experience, to see that in teachers."

The insight students gained from FDJ communication is not limited to the exchanges they have with their parents and teachers. Some students also felt they learned from other students' parents. Kelly, one of Amber's students, was friends with Lana and knew her dad, but had no idea that he spoke six languages, something she might never have learned if not for journal sharing.

Making Learning Meaningful

The journals gave students a forum in which they could deepen their learning and express opinions that they might not have articulated in an oral discussion. Amber's student Casey wrote, "Sometimes the given prompts were challenging to write about, but that forced me to think deeper and find real connections that I never would have." More than one student commented on the difficult nature of the subjects, but appreciated being encouraged to think "outside the box" or, as Amber would say, outside of their experience. Zuhair summed up students' reactions when he said that the prompts "really made me see how much I've grown as a person." Takaiyah, Stephanie's student, mentioned in her letter to her grandmother, "I do liked them cause I get those questions that strechs my brain." Jimmy, one of Angela's students, stated, "I realized that there is usually a way you can connect to something, no matter how far off it seems, and your peers and parents can make connections, too." Mary, another student in Angela's class, felt the FDJ helped her to become more self-reflective:

> It challenged me to think in ways I've never thought before and a lot of these questions got me thinking of myself as a person and what I really believe. I learned things about my sister, my mom, my dad, and you, Mrs. Dean, that I never knew before and my point of view changed for all of them for the better. I now understand more.

The FDJs help to bring students' lives to the center of the classroom, and students benefit from knowing that their thoughts and stories matter. In his reflection on favorite moments in Angela's class, Jimmy wrote:

> I liked how for the majority of the year we talked about real stuff and not just work out of the book. You were focused on getting us into it, not the information into us. You got us to think about things differently, which I try to do myself, but a little help never hurts.

FDJs were so meaningful and engaging, some of Jennifer's students planned their own extensions. Jazmin wrote, "Sience we've took'in everthing home we can see how you made it and see if we can make it." Elizabeth planned on "wirting dearing the somer to my Mom and Dad What I do in the Summer Camp."

As is to be expected, some students struggled to connect fully with the FDJs. A few of Stephanie's students discussed the challenge of actually writing a letter. They enjoyed the question-writing and finding out the answers but did not necessarily enjoy writing the letter each week describing their learning. One student said, "I don't like about it is when you have to write a letter instead of writing just the question." We encouraged students to share their honest opinions so that the class would improve upon the process throughout the year, but let's face it—if a student doesn't like to write, this may not be his or her favorite learning activity. So you might engage your class in an experiment. One week, everyone just writes a question instead of a full letter. Then, discuss the types of family responses from just questions as opposed to full letters. Or, study mentor texts to explore how your class's favorite informational writers compose their ideas.

THOUGHTS ON USING JOURNALS OVER TIME AND ACROSS GRADES

Journaling between families and children throughout the years can be a priceless connection and keepsake. One parent told Amber, "Thank you so much for thinking of such an awesome activity that involves the parents as well. Becky and I had to do a similar activity when she was in 1st grade and to finish her high school career by doing the same is just precious!" Zuhair's father expressed his desire to have the opportunity to see his son's progression in writing and how his opinions changed as he matured. He said, "It encourages creativity and develop of ideas between family members—a step very vital for the growing kids . . . I wish this journal was there for the whole high school years." Some students loved the journals so much that they wanted to continue them during the summer. Elyse created summer journals with her students. They made front and back covers from old cereal boxes and construction paper. Students used stickers, paint, photographs, magazines, or markers to decorate the cover. Elyse stapled sheets of paper between the covers and students took them home the last day of school.

But we have to question: What would happen if every classroom used dialogue journals? Would it become overwhelming? Imagine every student journaling in every class from kindergarten to high school graduation. How many journals is that? What about families with more than one child? What about secondary teachers and some elementary teachers who have more than one class? Much like Thanksgiving dinner, sometimes too much of a good thing is uncomfortable.

We have implemented and brainstormed many ideas for using journals over time, and know that our readers are wise teachers who will come up with additional strategies. Suggestions include the following:

1. For teachers of multiple classes, consider using journals for particular instructional units (a genre study, a major novel, a science inquiry) and stagger their use across classes. You do lose the cumulative growth potential however, since it takes students and families time to develop dialogue.
2. Alternatively, teachers with multiple classes might use journals with only one class (some of us did), or one first semester and a different one next semester.
3. Teams of teachers at the secondary level might alternate using journals across the year in different subjects. The students would be taking journals home weekly to share with families, but the focus might be social studies for the first 9 weeks, language arts the second 9 weeks, and so on.
4. A similar scenario might work for an elementary school that wants to implement Family Dialogue Journals schoolwide. For example, language arts might be the focus for the first 2 years, with other content foci at upper grade levels (e.g., 5th-grade dialogues about social studies topics).
5. For families with multiple children in FDJ classrooms, talk! What would work for you and your family? Are there family members other

than Mom or Dad who could respond some or all of the time, perhaps on a rotation system? Could you alternate weeks and children with longer and shorter responses?

6. Include art, music, physical education, media specialists, and other instructional support teachers as well as counselors, social workers, nurses, and psychologists. These educators may take segments of time throughout the year to initiate their own journal entries—for example, during a unit on protest music through the ages. Alternately, they may serve as journal correspondents for students who do not have anyone at home who is able to respond to their entries. We sometimes enlisted school staff such as secretaries, custodians, and others to serve this vital role in a child's FDJ experience.

7. Consider online journals—cautiously. Certainly it would be easier for the teacher to have the journals available online rather than carrying them home. Families would benefits from being able to access the journals wherever they might be, and from reading responses from other students and families. Smartphones are ubiquitous in high schools and being able to pull up the journal on their phones might lead to more consistent student participation. However—and this is a major concern—not all students and families have Internet access. Frustration with technology might actually decrease the number of regularly participating families. We also worry about privacy and whether families would create entries with the same depth and intimacy we experienced. While teachers told families that their journal entries might be shared aloud, a paper journal allows families and students to ask for privacy when necessary—and some did. Angela addressed these problems by making it an option for students to use email for their journals.

8. Make the journals multimodal. Using technology allows students and families to record oral responses or conversations and to add photos, videos, blog links, and even readings they've done in class. Even without computers, however, students and families across grade levels made the journals their own by drawing pictures, adding photographs, and sometimes creating graphics such as maps.

9. For parents or guardians who are uncomfortable with their own literacy, causing them to respond irregularly if at all, talk with them to create options. In our classrooms, this was sometimes the case. Usually there was someone in the family, either at home or in the extended family, who felt comfortable writing in the journals or writing for a parent who wanted to respond. In most cases above 2nd grade, students wrote for parents who were not literate. For older students with cellphones, parents could record their responses. In our experience, almost all families found a way to participate.

Sometimes, it might just seem like kids are tired of the journals, and they may be. Jen, her students, and their families committed themselves to dialogue journals for 2 academic years and, at times, faced journal fatigue. When the excitement eventually began to wane, they had to work together to identify changes. They adapted by sometimes skipping a week of writing to ensure everyone had plenty of time to share. They branched out into two topics each week so children had more of a choice in what they wrote to their families.

Yet these shifts were not enough. One Friday when she opened the discussion of what to write in the journal that week, a collective groan arose. Jen decided to spend their next Morning Meeting discussing how the children felt about FDJs in order to identify options for making the process more enjoyable.

"It seems that some of you might not be as excited about family journals as you used to be. What was it that is hard for you? Or that you don't like?" Jen asked.

The class looked a little nervous. No one spoke.

"Let's see," Jen continued. "We have decided to have different groups of you working on different questions. Do you still like that?"

They nodded.

"Okay. How about completing the journals every other week? Is that still something you like?"

More nodding.

"What about writing to your families? Do you still want to do that?"

Their heads shook up and down.

"Hmm," she pondered, "what else might be wrong?"

Denim's hand was up almost immediately. "There's never enough time," she said. "We always just get started, and it's time to clean up."

Now that the students were able to write for sustained periods, they had much more to write and not enough time in which to write it. Their conversations were also lengthier, as they decided on multiple topics so everyone had choices.

"Can't we use Writing Workshop time on Thursday *and* Friday to do home journals?" a small voice suggested.

"Yeah!" "I want to do that!"

Jen pondered. Since she and her students were now writing in their journals only once every *other* week, spending 2 days on each dialogue journal entry would be no more of a time commitment than previously. This plan would alleviate the pressure students felt, racing to write before the *beep, beep, beep* of the timer. Since so many teachers came to Jen's room to pull students out or teach lessons throughout the day, lengthening each session was not an option, which made the idea even more appealing.

"What do you think? Would you like to try this? Would you feel better about journals if you had more time each week to write in them?"

Nods and a chorus of "yes!" filled the air. The children, firm in their belief about the importance of sharing with their families, were able to collaboratively identify a solution. As the students and their abilities grew and changed, so did their Family Dialogue Journals and the process through which they wrote and shared them. Jen knew this might not be the last alteration she and the children would make, but seeing their ability to talk through and come to a solution gave her confidence that, if necessary, they would adjust again.

GOING FORWARD

The purpose of FDJs was to establish a dependable two-way communication channel between a caring adult in the school, the student, and home. Too often, Joseph noted, the care the student receives at school and that of home never make the connection in the form of ongoing, purposeful dialogue. Even more rarely does that dialogue include the student. Joseph advised that whether your position is that of school counselor, some form of interventionist, administrator, or teacher, the FDJ opens doors of opportunity for understanding and relationship building, which, as we all know, is critical in human development.

We acknowledge that FDJs may be easier to implement in some classrooms than others; this was true for us across classrooms and across years. For example, the majority of Amber's upper-middle-class, advanced high school students had college-educated parents who had played an active part in their students' education previously. Amber had a high participation rate in the FDJ project. However, so did the majority of us where the classrooms' demographics were quite different. Research suggests that many parents (especially families of color and those affected by poverty) do not communicate with the school because they feel that their voices are not welcome. The purpose behind the FDJs, to recognize that home and family experiences are indeed relevant to the classroom, may seem foreign to such families initially. While it may take more time to reach out to these parents to help them realize your genuine interest in their stories and perspectives, the evidence in this book shows it is worth the effort for students and their families.

As with anything worthwhile, there will be trial and error, pitfalls and setback. During such struggles, we tried to reflect and discuss with families, students, and other educators. Stephanie felt embarrassed her first year that the only introduction was a letter to parents glued to the front cover of the journal. She knew she could have done a better job modeling the process for the students and parents, so the next year she introduced FDJs during home visits so all the parties were involved in determining how to make the journals work for their family. Elyse plans on hosting a family journaling workshop, where families participate in an evening of journaling to begin the project next year. For all of us, the FDJs were a manifestation of a larger goal that we kept front and center: creating a dynamic family–school learning community.

In Jen's classroom, Family Dialogue Journals expanded students' beliefs about who was included in their learning community. From the beginning of their kindergarten year together, Jen would often think aloud during journal time. "Hmmmmm . . ." she would say, tapping her chin with her forefinger. "I wonder what our families would think about that?" And so they would ask their families what, in fact, they *did* think, and wait in anticipation for their responses.

These wonderings began to permeate many other conversations, as well.

"Let's ask our families about that!" Naldo suggested when he and his classmates had a question about how to spell a word in Spanish.

"Not all families think that way," Jorge gently reminded his friends when they began sharing how much they loved President Obama.

Jen and her students thought not only about the knowledge their families might contribute to classroom learning but also about whether or not school events honored families' ability to participate. When some children did not regularly return their FDJs, Jen and her students discussed the fact that families participate in different ways. They brainstormed reasons why families might find it difficult to respond, identifying nighttime work schedules, taking care of siblings, and holding multiple jobs. Having this discussion was important to Jen, because she did not want children whose families did not respond to feel slighted or embarrassed.

The children began applying this logic to a variety of classroom situations. When Jen announced upcoming nighttime music performances, PTO meetings, or curriculum nights, Christopher always raised his hand. "My dad can't come," he would say. "He works when I get home from school."

Jen explained that there were multiple ways for families to learn with them and often pointed to FDJs as an option with few time constraints. Christopher nodded, as did the rest of the class, and they worked together to identify shared learning options for families who could not attend nighttime activities. In time, Christopher began to recognize that even if his father were available for a school event, other families might have difficulty participating. When the class prepared invitations to a family cookout to celebrate all they had learned in 1st grade, Christopher's hand shot up. "My dad can come," he said, "but some moms and dads work in the daytime. They can't come."

Jen's students were incorporating families' perspectives into their learning, as well as critically analyzing the effectiveness of school activities based on families' ability to attend. This acknowledgment grew from early conversations around the inclusion of family backgrounds and thoughts during

FDJ conversations. By opening up classroom space to discuss the people in students' lives outside school, we as teachers enabled families to become a vital extension of the learning community.

Our wish for you and for ourselves is to be alert to the possibilities of learning with families, to reflect critically on our practices, and to embrace and learn from both the struggles and successes. Most importantly, we hope that you will delight in the stories, questions, advice, and companionship of weekly dialogue with students and families.

References

Allen, J. (2007). *Creating welcoming schools: A practical guide to home–school partnerships with diverse families.* New York, NY: Teachers College Press.

Allen, J. (2010). *Literacy in the welcoming classroom: Creating family–school partnerships that support student learning.* New York, NY: Teachers College Press.

Austen, J. (1995). *Pride and prejudice.* Mineola, NY: Dover Publications. (Original work published 1813)

Bega, D., Johnson, J., & Jasper, C. (2012, February). *Rethinking Title 1 parental involvement: Moving beyond a checklist of activities to a systemic plan for sustained family and community engagement.* Paper presented at Georgia's 2012 Statewide Family Engagement Conference, Athens, GA.

Choi, Y. (2003). *The name jar.* New York, NY: Dragonfly Books.

Cisneros, S. (1991). *The house on Mango Street.* New York, NY: Vintage Books.

Darder, A., Baltodano, M., & Torres, R. (Eds.). (2009). *The critical pedagogy reader* (2nd ed.). New York, NY: Routledge.

Davis, C., & Yang, A. (2005). *Parents and teachers working together.* Turner Falls, MA: Northeast Foundation for Children.

Deng, B., Deng, A., Ajak, B., & Bernstein, J. (2005). *They poured fire on us from the sky: The story of three lost boys from Sudan.* New York, NY: Public Affairs.

Dudley-Marling, C. (2009). Home-school literacy connections: The perceptions of African American and immigrant ESL parents in two urban communities. *Teachers College Record, 111*(7), 1713–1752. Retreived from www.tcrecord .org (ID Number: 15307)

Dunbar, P. L. (1896). "We wear the mask." Retrieved from www.poetryfoundation .org/poem/173467

Ehrenreich, B. (2002). *Nickel and dimed.* New York, NY: Henry Holt.

Eiseley, L. (1979). *The star thrower.* Fort Washington, PA: Harvest Books.

Faulkner, W. (1985). *As I lay dying.* New York, NY: Vintage Books. (Original work published 1930)

Freire, P. (1970). *Pedagogy of the oppressed.* New York, NY: Continuum.

Freire, P. (2005). *Teachers as cultural workers.* Boulder, CO: Westview Press.

Frye, D. (2009, July 10). Engaging parents beyond the parent conference by using a shared "parent journal." *Teachers College Record.* Retrieved from www.tcrecord .org (ID Number 15717)

Gonzáles, N., Moll, L., & Amanti, C. (Eds.). (2005). *Funds of knowledge: Theorizing practices in households, communities, and classrooms.* Mahwah, NJ: Lawrence Erlbaum.

Grimes, N. (2002). *Bronx masquerade.* New York, NY: Dial Books.

Haubegger, C. (1994). "I'm not fat, I'm Latina." *Essence Magazine, 25*(8), 48.

Henderson, A., & Mapp, K. (2002). *A new wave of evidence: The impact of school, family, and community connections on student achievement.* Austin, TX: Southwest Educational Development Laboratory.

Henkes, K. (2008). *Chrysanthemum.* New York, NY: Mulberry Books.

Kay, A., Neher, A., & Lush, L. (2010). Writing a relationship: Home–school journals. *Language Arts, 87*(6), 417–426.

Kim, D. K. (2004). *Same difference and other stories.* Marietta, GA: Top Shelf Productions.

Kriete, R. (2002). *The morning meeting book.* Turner Falls, MA: Northeast Foundation for Children.

Landgraf, J., Silverman, B., Owens, H. T., Spurlock, M., & Cutler, R. J. (Executive Producers). (2005). *30 days* [Television series]. Irving, TX: FX Networks.

Lester, H. (1990). *Tacky the penguin.* Boston, MA: Houghton Mifflin Harcourt.

Lyons, G. (1999). *Where I'm from, where poems come from.* Spring, TX: Absey.

McCourt, F. (1996). *Angela's ashes.* New York, NY: Scribner.

National Governors Association Center for Best Practices & Council of Chief State School Officers. (2010). *Common Core State Standards.* Washington, DC: Authors.

Paris, D. (2012). Culturally sustaining pedagogy: A needed change in stance, terminology, and practice. *Educational Researcher, 41*(3), 93–97.

Rodriguez, R. (1983). *Hunger of memory: The education of Richard Rodriguez.* New York, NY: Bantam Books.

Rosen, M. J. (Ed.). (1992). *Home: A collaboration of thirty distinguished authors and illustrators of children's books to aid the homeless.* New York, NY: HarperCollins.

Rowe, D., & Fain, J. (2013). The family backpack project: Responding to dual-language texts through family journals. *Language Arts, 90*(6), 402–416.

Rylant, C. (2000). *The old woman who named things.* Boston, MA: HMH Books for Young Readers.

Shakespeare, W. (2002). *Othello.* New York, NY: Oxford University Press. (Original work published 1604)

Shockley, B., Michalove, B., & Allen, J. (1995). *Engaging families: Connecting home and school literacy communities.* Portsmouth, NH: Heinemann.

Simmons, A. M. (2013). A dialogue of three: The use of family dialogue journals in the ELA classroom. In H. Kreider & M. Caspe (Eds.), *Promising Practices in Engaging Families in Literacy* (pp. 85–98). Newark, DE: International Reading Association.

Vasquez, V. M. (2004). *Negotiating critical literacies with young children.* Mahwah, NJ: Lawrence Erlbaum.

Weiss, H., Lopez, E., & Rosenberg, H. (2010). *Beyond random acts: Family, school, and community engagement as an integral part of education reform.* Boston, MA: Harvard Family Research Project.

Wilde, O. (2003). *The importance of being Earnest.* New York, NY: Barnes & Noble Classics. (Original work published 1895)

Wollman-Bonilla, J. (2000). *Family message journals: Teaching writing through family involvement.* Urbana, IL: National Council of Teachers of English.

Woodson, J. (2001). *The other side.* New York, NY: Putnam.

Index

A letter *t* after a page number indicates a table.

About the Authors

JoBeth Allen retired from the University of Georgia in 2014 where she loved teaching, writing, and codirecting the Red Clay Writing Project where all of us met. She relishes spending more time with her family, including grandchildren Grace, Luke, Mia, Cora, and Anikin. Her educational passion now is work with undocumented immigrant students pursuing higher education in the face of institutional and societal barriers.

Jennifer Beaty is a 3rd-grade teacher in Gwinnett County, Georgia, where she has been teaching for 10 of her 13 teaching years. She learned about FDJs in her graduate coursework at the University of Georgia and she couldn't imagine teaching without them. She loves to spend time with her husband, David, and their baby, Eli.

Angela Dean is a 9th- and 10th-grade English Language Arts teacher in Gwinnett County, Georgia, where she has taught for 13 years. Angela was a fellow in the 2007 invitational summer institute with the Red Clay Writing Project (RCWP) while finishing her master's degree in language and literacy education at the University of Georgia. As a teacher consultant, she found her professional voice with her RCWP colleagues through classroom study groups, and her work with FDJs began. When Angela is not teaching and mentoring students, she fills her breaks from school traveling with her husband, seeing live music, gardening, and loving on her three dogs.

Joseph Jones taught for 2 years as a middle school graduation coach, a role that combined counselor, tutor, academic coach, social worker, mentor, and community liaison in order to support students in reaching their full potential. He is now a personal trainer, applying his coaching skills in another arena. He has a degree in English from Purdue University.

Stephanie Smith Mathews is taking time away from teaching elementary school to be a stay-at-home mom. She couldn't bear to leave teaching completely, so she is an online instructor for BYU-Idaho. Stephanie completed her master's degree in language and literacy education at the University of Georgia, and this continues to be one of her favorite decisions. She currently lives in Utah and enjoys spending time with her family and dog in the beautiful outdoors.

Jen McCreight, a former kindergarten and 1st-grade teacher, is an assistant professor in early childhood education at Hiram College in Hiram, Ohio. Her research interests include building family-school partnerships in diverse school contexts and engaging with students and families around the way we use words in our world. She loves spending time with her daughter and husband, reading books, playing outside, stopping by the local donut shop, and visiting friends and family.

Amber M. Simmons earned her doctorate in language and literacy from the University of Georgia and currently teaches 11th-grade American literature and AP Language and Composition in Gwinnett County, Georgia. She also serves as an adjunct professor at Mercer University and Brenau University. Her research interests include critical literacy, systemic functional linguistics, and the use of popular culture in the classroom.

Elyse Schwedler received her undergraduate degree from Clemson University in elementary education and her master's degree in children's literature and language arts from the University of Georgia. Currently, she serves as an EIP teacher in an Atlanta area elementary school. She has previously taught kindergarten, 2nd grade, and English for Speakers of Other Languages. Elyse enjoys learning with and from teachers to improve her teaching practices. She has had the privilege of working with wonderful teachers and students in three different Georgia cities.